PIZZA
FROM THE
HEART

PIZZA FROM THE HEART

100 Recipes for Pies, Pasta, Salads, and More

■ ■ ■ ■ ■ ■ ■ ■ ■

Paulie Gee and Mary Ann Giannone

FOUNDERS OF PAULIE GEE'S

with Sarah Zorn

UNION
SQUARE
& CO.

NEW YORK

UNION SQUARE & CO. and the distinctive Union Square & Co. logo are trademarks of Sterling Publishing Co., Inc.

Union Square & Co., LLC, is a subsidiary of Sterling Publishing Co., Inc.

Text © 2025 Paulie and Mary Ann Giannone
Photographs © 2025 Matt Taylor-Gross

Vanilla Ice Cream on page 169 is from *Van Leeuwen Artisan Ice Cream*, © 2015 by Laura O'Neill, Ben Van Leeuwen, and Pete Van Leeuwen. Courtesy of HarperCollins Publishers.

ISBN 978-1-4549-5431-6
ISBN 978-1-4549-5432-3 (e-book)

For information about custom editions, special sales, and premium purchases, please contact specialsales@unionsquareandco.com.

Printed in China

10 9 8 7 6 5 4 3 2 1

unionsquareandco.com

Editor: Caitlin Leffel
Designer: Renée Bollier
Photographer: Matt Taylor-Gross
Food Stylist: Spencer Richards
Prop Stylist: Brooke Deonarine
Project Editor: Ivy McFadden
Production Manager: Terence Campo
Copy Editor: Mark McCauslin

Shutterstock.com: adehoidar: 232; Afanasia: 136; Aleachim: 67, 139, 215; Aust28: 64; Steve Collender: 89, 159, 235; ELENALime: 86; Anna Gar: 106, 156; mozz.art: 24; Sunnydream: 212; tomertu: 27, 109, 185; Vectorpocket: 182. Courtesy of Adam Kuban: 169

A portion of the proceeds from the sale of this book will be donated to food insecurity and children/teen mentoring programs.

We dedicate this book to all the dreamers willing
to take the risks required to pursue their passions.
We hope our story inspires you to toss conventional
wisdom to the curb, whether you're young enough
not to realize what you're getting yourself into
or old enough to know better.

CONTENTS

Jane Pauley did a story on us for CBS once. She referred to our late-to-the-game entrance into the pizza industry as being "smart, slow, and right." Well, hindsight is certainly 20/20. If you had met Paulie Gee and me at any point prior to today and watched us as we embarked on our dream of owning a small business, that word—"slow"—fit us perfectly. We were in our late forties and early fifties when it became clear the life we were leading no longer fit the people we had become. Of course, what we proceeded to realize was that our new life calling didn't always feel smart. And the unconventional way we entered the restaurant business certainly wasn't right . . . at least if we were looking to do it the way everyone else did it. However, in the end, we followed our instincts, and trusting in others and ourselves became our recipe for success.

—MARY ANN GIANNONE (AKA MRS. GEE)

What she said.

—PAUL GIANNONE (AKA PAULIE GEE)

IN THE BEGINNING . . .

We Complement Each Other.
He Cooks. She Can't.

Mary Ann Giannone: He approached me in a disco in Bay Ridge, Brooklyn, on November 12, 1976. He came up to me and said, "I know you. I see you on the RR train."[1]

And I said, "Likely story."

Paulie still insists he remembers the tan coat I wore to work. I asked him recently what would have happened if he hadn't seen me at the disco that night. He says he would have found me anyway. Wow, that really sounds like stalking, doesn't it?

Paul Giannone: I was working at the Port Authority at the time, taking the train to work every day. Mary Ann took the train, too. I used to see her, she caught my eye, but I wasn't gonna approach her on the train.

One night I was out with my friends, she was out with her friends. I walk by her in the disco and I say, "I know you. You take the RR." I asked her to dance a couple of times, but that was basically it. I intentionally paid more attention to her friends and ignored her the rest of the night. Then I think I ended up driving them home . . .

MG: You went home with us in a car service. You didn't have a car.

PG: Okay, they wanted me to pay for a cab, so they dragged me along. Her friend shoved Mary Ann's telephone number in my hand on the way out of the car. So I called her up and we went for a burger one day. That's how we met.

MG: Forty-eight years ago.

PG: I can't find anybody better. Everybody's taken already.

MG: We never tell each other what to do, is really what it is. We never have. I think that's why we have such a long-lasting relationship, because we give each other a lot of room. But we've always encouraged one another to go after things and improve. To be the best we can be. Because we're not threatened. I'm certainly not threatened by him, and he sure isn't threatened by me.

Hitting the Not-a-Geek
Glass Ceiling.

PG: I was an employee of AT&T for eighteen years. I wasn't all that good at what I did, okay? I wasn't a geek, but I chose a career as a geek. Which meant that I was competing with people who did it well and loved it.

In 2001, at the age of forty-eight, I decided to move into consulting. But since I couldn't find work in the Tri-State area, I was always traveling to places like Houston, Texas, which is where I was when the planes crashed into the Twin Towers, by the way. I couldn't go home, and my family was alone in New Jersey throughout that horrible time. I'd come home on the weekends when I could handle the idea of getting on a plane again, but it definitely wasn't fun.

MG: What was fun for Paulie was cooking. And I enjoyed entertaining. For years, friends would tell Paulie he should open a restaurant, to which he responded, "I want no part of it." This may be one of the funniest things he's ever said.

---

1   See, this was so long ago that the RR train doesn't even exist anymore.

PG: Well, making pizza is a far different process than running a restaurant. You chop up toppings, you put them on the dough, you stick them in the oven.

Anyway, in my free time, I'd become infatuated with coal-burning pizza, wood-fired pizza. I started touring around to different spots and found people like Mark Iacono from Lucali, who was a marble-countertop fabricator before he became the owner of the most popular pizza place in NYC. That showed me right there . . . this is something I could accomplish. Someone who didn't know about pizza and wasn't in the business was able to become successful. It emboldened me to take a chance. I decided to build an oven in the backyard of my New Jersey home just to prove to myself that I could do it, and we went from there.

You Better Still Have Your Two Hands When I Get Back.

MG: Paulie went online, found plans for an oven, then started building it in the yard. Quite frankly, I got nervous, because he's not a very handy person. If I ever saw him with some sort of tool or paintbrush in our house . . . well, let's just say I would wonder what in the world was going on.

Anyway, when he rented a brick cutter and brought it home, that's when I knew he was serious. Because he did not operate heavy machinery. So when I left him that day, I said, "Okay, but you better still have your two hands when I get back."

Well, we began throwing weekly pizza-tasting parties in November 2007, since everyone has always loved our parties. And we did this for about two years with our little backyard oven, making one

pie at a time. We'd play music and hand out our housemade limoncello.

PG: I'd always enlist someone to keep the oven hot while I did the prep work inside, and some people were better than others. Typically it was Yankees fans, and not Mets fans.

MG: Paulie always, always shopped for everything, because he's very particular about any ingredient he uses in his food. But we cleaned up together, and I kind of assisted as a sous-chef, although Paulie hates that term because he hates being coined as a chef. He just hates it. If you're a doctor, you're a doctor, but a chef? People write stuff to Paulie and call him "Chef," and we just laugh because he hates it so much.

PG: At first, I just used dough from Stop & Shop. Then I graduated to making my own dough using my father-in-law's Pillsbury breadmaker.

MG: That breadmaker is on display in the restaurant to this day, by the way.

PG: I'd try different hydrations on the dough, different fermentation times, different toppings. I kept experimenting and experimenting and posting pictures on social media as I went along. And I began putting together a business plan. I mean, I didn't have any money at the time, just bills. But as soon as I built the oven, I started telling people I was going to open a pizzeria. I didn't give myself an option to back out because once you make a commitment like that, you need to follow through.

We Gotta Tawk.

PG: It became my goal to get influential people to try my pizza and have them say nice things about it. Like Joshua Levin, cocreator of the blog *GoodEater*. He'd written an article about the owner of a chile farm in South Africa who'd built a wood-burning oven that he essentially used to keep his family and all of his workers fed. At the end of the article, Josh asked people to write in about anyone they knew who had a pizza-oven lifestyle. So in the comments section I wrote, "Josh, we gotta tawk."

I posted pictures of my own oven, and in minutes, we were going back and forth. Next thing you know, I invited him to come to my house for a pizza tasting. It was on Thanksgiving weekend of 2008, and it was great. Josh brought his father, his brother, some neighbors, and some guy dressed in a kilt. He wrote about it on his blog, and Adam Kuban, the founder of the blog *Slice*, reposted the article, saying that Josh had "scored" an invite to a Paulie Gee's pizza tasting. Just like that, I was desirable!

We eventually had Adam over, too, along with Scott Wiener from Scott's Pizza Tours, and a lot of the other top bloggers at the time. Got 'em drunk first on my homemade limoncello, so my pizza tasted better. That got the ball rolling, and I was doing what I loved to do. Feeding people, talking to them, playing music for them. We'd try to invite eight people because we cut our pies in eighths. Which is my only regret. In retrospect, we should have cut them into sixths. The slices were too small.

Investing Half in the Business, Half in Sleep Medication.

MG: Going into this, Paulie never wanted to owe anyone money. That was the main thing. So we got a group of investors together—mostly friends and family—that threw in about 5K, 15K each. So not a lot. And we took out a home equity loan because people wanted to see that we had skin in the game, too.

PG: Everyone asked me the same question: "You want my money, what about your money?" At first I ignored them, moved on, called them jerks for even asking me that question. But I knew I had to do something. I wasn't exactly setting the world on fire in corporate IT. So I did what I had to do: Took out a home equity loan, used half of it as seed money, then put the other half aside for a rainy day because things invariably go sideways.

MG: It was the same then as it is now. We don't have funding, we're not part of a restaurant group, no one is going to catch us if we fall. When you have your own business, you just have to get up and get going and keep moving. So when we took the leap that we were going to do this, all we could do was follow through. Although I did keep my own full-time job for years.

PG: Originally I thought I was going to keep my day job as a safety net, too, and open the pizza place somewhere nearby in New Jersey. But when it came to investors, I knew they weren't going to trust us if I wasn't fully focused on the business because I was worried about some other job. So I quit, long story short. Otherwise, this story could end up going on for a long time.

Artists, Musicians, and Tattoos. That's My Holy Trinity.

PG: Once I realized that I didn't need to be close to my other job in New Jersey, I started looking for spaces in Brooklyn. I wanted to open up in Williamsburg, but Williamsburg is very expensive. And besides, two of the biggest names in NYC pizza were already there, Fornino and Motorino. They had been helpful to me during this process, by the way, and I didn't want to step on their toes. So I figured I had to find the next neighborhood, like Roberta's did with Bushwick. And Greenpoint was the next next neighborhood.

I picked the brain of a guy I knew who lived over there, and I used the "h" word. Are there any hipsters in Greenpoint? Do these hipsters ride bicycles? He said absolutely, so I decided to give it a look. And I saw cool beer bars like Brouwerij Lane scattered between the dollar stores. There were bars, but not many places to eat. Perfect.

There was a former restaurant space at 60 Greenpoint Avenue that had burned down and closed, but there was no "for rent" sign or anything. So I tracked down the landlord. The second I walked into the space, I knew I was home. The landlord tried to tell me that there was someone else interested in the space, and that they wanted to put the same concept in. I didn't know if he was full of it or not, but I wasn't going to take a chance.

So I took the space and it was the scariest day of my life. But I asked God for wisdom, strength, and courage, and like most of the times in my life that I've asked, I received that help. Did I ask for a lottery ticket win, too? Yeah, I did. But I can't blame that loss on God.

We're Not Businesspeople. We're People People.

PG: One of the best bits of advice I got was from the legendary Chris Bianco, when I asked if he thought I should make my own mozzarella. His answer was, "You're in New York. There are about a million guys here who make fresh mozzarella better than you could. Support them, and they'll support you. That way everyone wins."

So I started looking for local products that I could use. Poor Mary Ann—she's heard this story a million times.

MG: What do you mean, heard it? I lived it.

PG: There was this monthly food market in Greenpoint at the time that was sort of like a roadshow. It popped up in different places like church basements, and featured independent food artisans selling their wares. It became so popular, they made the cover of the *New York Times*'s Sunday Style section. But you know who else reads the *New York Times*? The Health Department. And they shut them down.

I had been using this great bacon marmalade I'd found there on my pies, so I invited the maker, Ross, to cook his product in my kitchen instead of in his home. Eventually, I did the same with Mike of Mike's Hot Honey, which went on to become a really successful product. And in turn, those products became a differentiator for us.

MG: We have to run a business, pay bills, all of those things. But at the end of the day, it's really about the people . . . the people employed by us and the people who come in. That's been our focus from the very beginning. Everyone has different roles, but everyone is valuable.

With a lot of businesses, you don't even know who the owners are. But we're not hiding behind the scenes. We're up front every night, talking to our guests, learning about our guests . . .

PG: Sometimes, we even recommend other pizza places to our guests.

MG: At the beginning, we took the value of that for granted, but it's something we've become known for, and that people really appreciate.

Listen, we didn't go to college for a degree in hospitality. But we know hospitality. It's something that's innate. And by making the effort to connect with our community, we built on the synergy of the neighborhood at the time. There were lots of artists and people starting out. There was a lot of energy here and a desire to support one another. Basically, we were at the right place at the right time.

Something Is Going to Stress You Out in Life. It Might as Well Be Something You Love.

PG: We believe that you can help yourself by helping other people. And I like helping career-change people. I owed it to my investors and to my brand to expand, but I didn't want to run multiple locations. So after talking to a whole bunch of lawyers, we decided to start a franchise company.

MG: Our structure is very loose and very different from regular franchises. For starters, we know all the people we work with; we know their stories and their families. And while we start with a template of what we'd like to see at each franchise, we also give owners room to create their own recipes that mean something to them

and that'll work in the area they're in. For instance, in Chicago, they've got Chinese-inspired pies and Filipino-style pies that are based on the owners' cultures.

PG: The only time things didn't work out was when one franchisee wanted to use Pandora instead of my playlist. That was a deal-breaker.

MG: And in addition to the franchises, we started opening slice shops, which really saved us during the pandemic. The wood-fired pies at 60 Greenpoint weren't built to travel. So the slice shops allowed us to stay open in some capacity, even if it was just for takeout and delivery. We can survive any circumstance.

PG: After finally realizing how my heart and mind operates, and how I feel when I'm working for myself and doing what I believe in, I could never work for somebody else again. I could NOT go to work for somebody else. That ship has sailed. That ship has sunk.

It's easy for me to take whatever the business throws at me because I'm living my best life. And Mary Ann is living her best life. I get to do what I like to do, which is make pizza and promote other people, and Mary Ann gets to do what she likes to do, which is to be charitable and work with the community. So we're doing what we love and we've gotten everything we've asked for. Except we still don't have a pizzeria at the beach.

PAULIE'S PANTRY

These are the items you'll always want to keep on hand for making pizza. Although I hope I don't need to tell you not to actually store cheese and meat in your pantry—the alliteration just sounded good.

Note for vegans: If you're vegan, you probably already have your favorite go-to brands, but we like Follow Your Heart parm, NUMU mozzarella, and Mellody honey.

FLOUR + YEAST

All-purpose flour: For breading, and other uses.

Breadcrumbs: My favorite brand is 4C, either plain or seasoned, depending on what the recipe calls for.

Caputo 00 flour: This is a finer, softer grind of flour that's high in protein. It's ideal for making dough for Neapolitan-style pies, which have a slow rise and cook at high temperatures.

Instant yeast: I like SAF, but the brand is less important than making sure you're using instant yeast and not active dry yeast.

King Arthur bread flour: Bread flour is high in protein and gluten, and is responsible for the thicker, sturdier dough that you'll find in Sicilian, Grandma, and classic NY-style pies.

Semolina: This prevents your pizza dough from sticking to your table, peel, stone, and other surfaces, and doesn't burn in the oven like flour would.

CHEESES

Fresh mozzarella: We almost always use fresh whole-milk mozzarella for Neapolitan-style pies. It's more flavorful, more delicate, and does best under quick, high heat. Otherwise it gets soupy.

Shredded low-moisture mozzarella: This is for classic NY-style pies or pizza made in a conventional oven. It's a great melter, isn't overly salty, and won't get the crust soggy. Always use whole-milk mozz, never part-skim.

Parmigiano Reggiano and Pecorino Romano: These are both hard Italian grating cheeses with similar flavor profiles, but Parm is delicate and pecorino is more robust.

Ricotta: Always high-quality whole-milk ricotta.

MEATS

Guanciale: This is cured pork jowls or cheeks, and it's rich and fatty and salty. Why bother to use salt in your dishes when you have guanciale? It's similar to bacon in consistency, but is unsmoked.

Prosciutto di Parma: Prosciutto is a thinly sliced cured Italian ham that's delicate and nutty. We only ever put it on our pizza post-oven, because it loses all of its best qualities when it's cooked or crisped.

Soppressata: We especially like hot soppressata (soppressata piccante) for the kick. It's like an upscale pepperoni, with globs of fat throughout instead of little bits.

OTHER STAPLES

Olive oil: I use regular olive oil both for making dough and drizzling on pizza before it goes into the oven. Extra-virgin olive oil (EVOO) is the good stuff and its primary purpose is flavor. I use it for post-oven pizza applications.

Fine sea salt: When I do call for salt (see the sidebar below), it's sea salt, which I mostly use as a finishing touch or for seasoning pasta water.

Butter: Salted butter, mostly. It adds umami. Particularly good on pizza crusts.

Canned Italian plum tomatoes: If you happen to have a friend in food service, ask them to get you Alta Cucina brand for whole tomatoes, and Tomato Magic for ground tomatoes. You can also order them online. Otherwise, go for the best-quality brand of whole peeled Italian-style tomatoes that you can find in a grocery store, like Sclafani. It's a popular one these days because of the nice label. You can puree the tomatoes and put them on pizza just like that, unless we're talking about vegan pies. For those, I'll cook the pureed tomatoes into a sauce for extra umami.

Clams: Fresh, if you can afford them, but there's nothing wrong with a good brand of canned chopped clams.

Anchovies: Canned are fine—it's too much work to deal with fresh anchovies.

Dried pasta: We prefer the De Cecco brand. It's high-quality and reliable, and I don't like to be surprised. You can find all sorts of fancy Italian brands in the supermarket nowadays, but I'm not about to start experimenting. Favorite shapes are rigatoni, perciatelli (which is hard to find—you might have to substitute bucatini), thin spaghetti or linguine fini, and penne rigate. Pappardelle is the only instance where fresh is better, because of how eggy and tender it is. That, and ravioli from local purveyors. Avoid frozen pasta whenever possible.

WE GOTTA TALK ABOUT SALT

Before you start cooking from this book, it's important that we have a little conversation about using salt. In that I don't. Not really. Other than in hot water for pasta. My grandmother never cooked much with salt, and I don't either. I'm just generally not big on putting extra stuff on food.

I'm more about letting the saltiness from the other ingredients I use take over. Take our NY-style pizzas: Most people will salt their tomatoes. I do not do that. I use aged low-moisture mozzarella, which is already salted. I like letting the slight sweetness of the tomatoes blend with the saltiness of the cheese, and do not do anything extra to mess that up.

Another reason I don't really like salt is that I really like consistency. And basically, I don't want to have to rely on some of the members in my kitchens to salt things properly. Salt is a matter of personal taste. So my overall note here is to season things to your own taste. And don't expect me to do it for you.

PAULIE'S PIZZA PRIMER

Making pizza at home—and not just in a conventional oven—has become a pretty popular activity. Everyone seems to have some sort of setup in their backyard. Maybe not a full-on wood-burning stove like I had, but at least an Ooni pizza oven or a similar brand like that. You don't even need a huge outdoor space, just a terrace will do. Breville has even come out with a wood-burning-style oven you can stick on a countertop.

That said, you can't just purchase some fancy wood-burning or propane oven and call it a day. And it takes a bit of know-how to get the most out of a conventional oven, too. There's a lot to consider when you're making pizza for a wood-burning or propane oven versus a conventional one, from the dough you use to what you put on top of it.

NEAPOLITAN-STYLE PIES

- **Oven:** Conventional home oven or outdoor wood-burning/propane oven

- **Temperature:** 550°F or as high as it will go for a conventional oven; 900°F minimum for an outdoor oven

- **Time in Oven:** 6 to 8 minutes (conventional oven); 60 to 90 seconds (outdoor oven)

A NOTE ON NEAPOLITAN VS. NY-STYLE PIZZA

Our restaurants make wood-fired Neapolitan-style pies, while our Slice Shops make NY-style pies. Neapolitan uses 00 flour, which is much finer than regular flour. They are cooked in a wood-burning oven at extremely high temperatures, typically 900° to 1,000°F. They are typically 12-inch pies and served whole.

NY-style is a larger format (our pies are 20 inches) and meant to be cut into eight slices. Pies are made using bread flour or all-purpose flour and are cooked at a lower temperature, typically around 600°F, which gives them a chewier consistency. Since conventional ovens max out at around 550°F, this is generally an easier style to make at home.

TOPPINGS

Shredded low-moisture whole-milk mozzarella is preferable when cooking pizza in a conventional home oven. Fresh mozzarella tends to get wet and soupy unless cooked quickly at high temperatures, which is exactly what makes it ideal for wood-burning and propane preparations. That said, there are a lot fewer rules about what other toppings you can put on a conventional oven–baked pizza, due to the lower, slower cooking. Since wood-burning ovens burn so hot and cook so quickly, certain toppings should only go on your pizza post-baking, including ricotta, honey, prosciutto, and speck. These are delicate ingredients, and extreme heat ruins them. It changes their character.

METHOD

You can use any stretching routine you're comfortable with, but at the restaurant we use a method that we affectionately call the Egyptian, because an Egyptian pizza maker showed it to me. As you're stretching the dough, you let a little less than half of the dough round hang off the side of the counter, so gravity helps stretch it. As you turn it a bit at a time, you keep part of the dough hanging off the counter until it's evenly stretched all the way around.

TOOLS

- Semolina, to keep the dough from sticking.
- A dough scraper for removing the dough from the container after proofing.
- A dough knife for portioning the dough.
- A big wooden placing peel for building the pizza on, preferably with slots in the bottom so you can shake off any extra semolina.
- A pizza stone or steel for the floor of your oven.
- A small turning peel or banjo peel for rotating the pizza in the oven and removing it when it's done.
- A wheel-type pizza cutter.
- A pizza-cutter sharpener, which is inexpensive and worth having.

Recipe for Success: Pizza

Proper proofing results in a light, airy, and delicious pizza. Underproofed dough will result in a dense, heavy, and less desirable pizza.

Neapolitan-Style Dough

Makes enough dough for
five 12-inch pies

When I started out making pizza at home, I used store-bought dough. Hey, I never claimed to be a baker. I eventually developed a dough for the restaurant, but keep in mind, we have a custom Stefano Ferrara wood-burning oven that cooks pizza in 1 minute flat at 900°F.

I made this dough recipe for the home cook to work with whatever oven you happen to have. No, it's not 100% identical to what you'd get at our restaurant, but then again, what is?

> 2 cups cold water
>
> 1 tablespoon fine sea salt
>
> 5 cups (625 g) 00 flour, such as Caputo or King Arthur
>
> ½ teaspoon instant yeast
>
> 2 teaspoons olive oil, plus more for greasing
>
> 1 cup semolina, for dusting

In a large bowl, combine the water and salt and stir to dissolve the salt. Using your hands or a spoon, mix in the 00 flour and yeast until the dough comes together. Cover the bowl with a damp towel and let the dough rest for 15 to 30 minutes. Give it a poke with your finger—if it bounces back quickly, it's ready. If not, it should rest awhile longer.

Drizzle in the oil, kneading the dough as you go to combine. Knead until the dough is smooth and springy, then cover with the towel and let rest for 5 minutes. Meanwhile, lightly oil five 1-quart lidded containers, sized to fit the dough snugly.

Divide the dough into 5 equal pieces and roll each into a seamless ball. Place each ball into one of the oiled containers, cover, and refrigerate for at least 1 day or up to 3 days. (To freeze for later use, see sidebar, page 21.) Bring the dough to room temperature before using.

Lightly dust a wooden pizza peel and your counter with some of the semolina. Lightly dust your hands back and front with semolina as well. Lift 1 dough ball out of its container with a dough scraper. Place the dough on the counter, making sure to keep the top side up. Gently press down in the middle of the dough with your fingertips and work toward the edge, stopping about an inch short of the edge. Turn the dough a quarter turn and repeat, pressing with your fingertips three times. Turn the dough over and repeat the four steps, then turn it over again and toss the dough back and forth from palm to palm as it continues to grow in size, keeping track of which side is the top.

Place your fists under the dough and gently stretch it with your fists, turning it a bit as you go. Repeat a few times and place the dough back on the counter, top-side up. Finally, hang half of the dough, but no more than that, over the edge of the counter, keeping the dough in place with the palms of your hands.

Rotate the dough with the palms of your hands until it stretches to the desired size, then place it on the prepared peel. Now you're ready to top your pie and bake it. If you're baking more than one pizza, forming each pie after the previous pizza is cooked.

NOTE

It is very important to dust your pizza peel with semolina and not the flour you used to make the dough. The 00 flour will burn in the oven, but the semolina will not.

SICILIAN, GRANDMA, AND NY-STYLE PIES

- **Oven:** Conventional indoor ovens
- **Temperature:** As high as it will go (550°F+)
- **Time in Oven:** 10 to 12 minutes

A NOTE ON PAN PIZZA (SICILIAN AND GRANDMA-STYLE)

We serve Sicilian and Grandma-style pizzas at our Slice Shops, both of which are cooked in pans rather than directly on the heating surface. A Sicilian's crust is fluffier and focaccia-like, due to a longer rising time; a Grandma's is crispy and thin.

We use steel pans with a 1-inch lip for both types of pies, but coated aluminum pans (such as Lloyd brand) are a good option for home cooks. Since a Grandma's crust is so thin, in a pinch you can use a baking sheet; just be sure to check the top and bottom of the pizza while it cooks to prevent it from burning.

It's great to have a pizza stone or steel for any style of pie when you're using a home oven, since it encourages hotter, more even cooking. Either place the pizza directly on the stone or steel for a NY-style pie, or place the pan on the stone if making a Sicilian or Grandma-style pizza.

TOPPINGS

You can be a bit more generous with the toppings than you would with a Neapolitan pie because the dough is thick and sturdy enough to handle them. And the lower heat means you can be more adventurous with the toppings because there's less chance of burning. It's better to use shredded low-moisture mozz than fresh, though, since it melts more evenly and won't make the pizza wet.

Recipe for Success: Pizza

Long cold fermentation time (up to 48 hours) is preferable for more flavorful and digestible dough.

METHOD

To maximize heat, always cook your pizza on a pizza stone or steel on the floor of your oven. If you're cooking in a pan, put the pan on the stone or steel, too. Home ovens tend to run at different temperatures, so keep an eye on your pizza to gauge the proper cook time and make sure it doesn't burn.

TOOLS

- A pizza stone or steel—a lot of professionals prefer steel, which holds and conducts heat better, isn't breakable, and can be easier to clean.

- A wooden pizza peel, if you're cooking directly on a stone or steel instead of in a pan.

- A pizza screen for reheating your pizza, which lifts it from the oven floor so it doesn't burn.

- Lloyd pans with a 1-inch lip for Sicilian- or Grandma-style pizzas (you can also use a baking sheet for Grandma pies).

HOW TO FREEZE PIZZA DOUGH

Wrap each ball of dough tightly in plastic wrap and place in a freezer bag. Freeze for up to 6 months. Before using, defrost the dough in the refrigerator overnight, then let it warm up to room temperature for about 4 hours. Timing will vary based on the temperature in your kitchen, so be sure that it's thawed completely before using. (The dough can be stored in the freezer for up to 6 months.)

NY-Style Dough

Makes enough dough for
two 14-inch pies

NY-style dough (also used for Grandma pies) and Sicilian dough are made with the same ingredients in different amounts. The Sicilian dough has a higher ratio of water to flour than NY-style dough.

  1⅓ cups warm water (70°F)
  ½ teaspoon instant yeast
  4 cups (530 g) bread flour, such as King Arthur
  1½ teaspoons fine sea salt
  2¼ teaspoons olive oil, plus more for greasing
  Semolina, for dusting

In the bowl of a stand mixer fitted with the dough hook, combine the water, yeast, and flour and mix on low speed for 4 minutes. Slowly add the salt and mix for 2 minutes more, until the dough is shiny. Slowly add the oil and mix for 4 minutes. Raise the mixer speed to high and knead for 1 minute, until the dough pulls away from the sides of the bowl.

Transfer the dough to a lightly oiled work surface. Divide the dough into two equal pieces (they should weigh about 430 g each). Shape the dough into balls and lightly coat the top of each ball with oil. Place each ball of dough in a separate bowl and cover with plastic wrap. Refrigerate for at least 24 hours or up to 48 hours. (To freeze for later use, see sidebar, page 21.)

Remove the dough from the refrigerator 3 hours before baking and let it sit at room temperature. About 45 minutes before baking, place a pizza stone or steel on the oven floor and preheat the oven to 550°F or as high as it will go.

Lightly dust a wooden pizza peel with semolina (see Note, page 20). Stretch one ball of the dough into a 14-inch round on top of the prepared peel. Top and bake. Repeat with the remaining dough, if desired.

Sicilian-Style Dough

Makes enough dough for
one 11 × 17-inch rectangular pie

  4¾ cups (570 g) bread flour, such as King Arthur
  1¾ cups warm water (70°F)
  ¾ teaspoon instant yeast
  2¼ teaspoons fine sea salt
  1 tablespoon olive oil, plus more for greasing
  Sesame seeds, for sprinkling

In the bowl of a stand mixer fitted with the dough hook, combine the flour, water, and yeast and mix on low speed for 4 minutes. Slowly add the salt and mix for 2 minutes, until the dough is shiny. Slowly add the oil and mix to incorporate. Raise the mixer speed to high and knead for about 1 minute, until the dough pulls away from the sides of the bowl.

Transfer the dough to a lightly oiled work surface. Gently stretch and flatten the dough slightly to facilitate handling. Fold the dough halfway toward its center. Take the opposite end and overlap it over the first fold. Rotate the dough and repeat the folding process. The end product should resemble a small, oily, well-formed pillow. Let sit at room temperature for 30 minutes.

Place the dough in a lightly oiled proofing box or large bowl and refrigerate for 24 hours.

Oil an 11 × 17-inch baking pan and sprinkle with sesame seeds. Carefully remove the dough from the box or bowl so you don't tear or damage it and place it on the prepared pan. Press the dough firmly into the pan, ensuring that there are no air bubbles and the dough is evenly distributed. Stretch the dough so it completely covers the pan and touches the edges.

Lightly oil the top of the dough to prevent sticking and cover with plastic wrap. Let proof until it is close to touching the plastic wrap, 3 to 4 hours. The dough is now ready to top and bake.

························

CHAPTER ONE

PLEASED TO MEAT YA

"You have to have a dream to have a dream come true."

How else would we kick things off, other than with a chapter devoted to the pies that define Paulie Gee's? Yes, the Hellboy is here. You're welcome. Many of these pies were created in our backyard oven, long before we opened the restaurant, while others were developed together with our staff members as Paulie Gee's grew.

In case you hadn't guessed it, all of the pies in this chapter contain meat. Keep flipping for the vegetarian and vegan pies. We have so many, they deserved their own chapter, too.

One of the signatures of a Paulie Gee's pie is the combination of sweet and savory. I start with one and figure out how to balance it with the other. Speck and pickled pineapple. Prosciutto and dried cherries. And, of course, Berkshire soppressata piccante with hot honey.

I also take inspiration from things I've tasted at other restaurants. I'm always thinking, How can I make that into a pie? Anise & Anephew came from this great swordfish with anisette cream sauce my friend ordered once. I wanted to stay true to that sauce, so I paired it with fennel and guanciale. Needless to say, the swordfish got the boot.

Lemon juice is big in my pies, too; it's amazing what it can do to contrast savory ingredients if you don't want to use sweet ingredients. Sadly, it doesn't always work. The greatest name I ever had for a pie had to be taken off the menu very quickly. It was a pie with spaghetti squash and lemon juice, which sounded good in theory but tasted wrong in reality. I called it the Sergio Limone, after Sergio Leone, the spaghetti Western director. If you know Paulie Gee's, you know that clever names are a huge part of our schtick.

Speaking of names, I came up with a pie that had four cheeses on it, and the last thing I was going to do was call it the Quattro Formaggi, like every other pizza place. So what did I call it? "Not the Quattro Formaggi." Being a little different than others is an element of what I do in and of itself.

Finally, a Paulie Gee's pie is all about balance. Balancing ingredients is essential. You never want to be overwhelmed by one flavor. Sometimes we cut back sauce if a pie is too wet or tomato forward. We dollop our ricotta just so. And I'm in a constant struggle with my pizza makers over how they disperse arugula. You can be pretty generous if you're making a Greenpointer, because arugula is supposed to be the star of the show. But with the Ricky Ricotta, you gotta go easy or you'll kill the pie.

I used to have a tomato sauce–only pie called the Simply Red, where guests could add whatever ingredients they wanted. THAT was a very bad idea. Sometimes people do stupid things to pizza, and I don't want them to have a bad experience because of it. So to this day, staff members have to consult with me first if a guest wants to make an off-menu addition to a pie. And I'll make a judgment call from there. **—PG**

Paulie's Playlist

"Feel Like Makin' Love," Bad Company

"Monte Cristi," Pedro Guzmán

"Every Hungry Woman," Allman Brothers Band

"Treat," Santana

"Lost on 23rd Street," Johnny Hammond

"Places and Spaces," Donald Byrd

"Walk Away from Love," David Ruffin

"Super Strut," Deodato

PLEASE READ BEFORE CONTINUING

All the OG PG's pies in this chapter and the following one are designed to be made in a conventional home oven using NY-Style Dough (page 22). To adapt for a wood-burning or propane oven, use Neapolitan-Style Dough (page 19), and swap out the shredded low-moisture mozzarella for fresh mozzarella. When making pizza in your home oven, set a pizza stone or steel on the floor of the oven and preheat the oven to 550°F or as high as it will go for 45 minutes. Use a semolina-dusted paddle to transfer the pie to the stone or steel. Bake for 6 to 8 minutes, until the crust is evenly brown and crisp and the cheese begins to brown slightly. Slice and serve.

DELBOY

Makes one 12-inch pie

I stole this pie from Motorino, who stole it from another Brooklyn pizzeria, Fornino. And we named it after our son, Derek, in the Paulie Gee's tradition of naming pies after family, friends, and employees.

Our son's nickname, Delboy, came from the British owner of a Colorado café. We were driving to the mountains for a ski trip and popped in for breakfast. The owner was a big talker, very gregarious, and when introduced to Derek, he pointed to him and said, "Where I'm from, you're Del Boy." It wasn't until much later that I learned it's the nickname of a character on an iconic British TV series called *Only Fools and Horses*. I'd never made the connection. I just figured that in England, it was like how if you're named Robert, you're called Bob. —**PG**

- -

1 round NY-Style Dough (page 22) or your favorite pizza dough (about ½ pound)

Semolina, for dusting

¾ cup pureed peeled fresh tomatoes or canned whole peeled Italian-style tomatoes

3 ounces shredded low-moisture mozzarella cheese

Grated Parmigiano Reggiano cheese, for sprinkling

16 thin slices soppressata piccante

Place a pizza stone or steel on the floor of your oven. Preheat the oven to 550°F or as high as it will go for 45 minutes.

Place the dough on a pizza paddle that's been dusted with semolina and stretch it to about 12 inches. Spread the pureed tomatoes evenly over the dough. Evenly scatter the mozzarella on top, then sprinkle with Parmigiano to cover. Space the soppressata slices evenly over the pie.

Use the paddle to transfer the pie to the pizza stone or steel on the floor of your oven. Bake for 6 to 8 minutes, until the crust is evenly brown and crisp and the cheese begins to brown slightly. Slice and serve.

RICKY RICOTTA

Makes one 12-inch pie

Whenever possible, I like our pie names to have a musical theme. In Ricotta da Vida made sense here. And eventually, we came up with a vegan version of the pie and decided to call it In Ricotta da Vegan (page 102).

We quickly came to realize there was too much opportunity to mistake one for the other, and certainly didn't want to serve the In Ricotta da Vida to a vegan, or the In Ricotta da Vegan to someone with a nut allergy. One of 'em needed to be changed, and so, on the advice of a friend, the nonvegan pie became the Ricky Ricotta. —PG

• •

⅓ cup crumbled sweet Italian fennel sausage (about 1 link, casing removed)

1 round NY-Style Dough (page 22) or your favorite pizza dough (about ½ pound)

Semolina, for dusting

¾ cup pureed peeled fresh tomatoes or canned whole peeled Italian-style tomatoes

Pecorino Romano cheese, for sprinkling

Whole-milk ricotta cheese, for dolloping

1 small handful of arugula

Extra-virgin olive oil, for drizzling

Place a pizza stone or steel on the floor of your oven. Preheat the oven to 550°F or as high as it will go for 45 minutes.

In a large skillet, cook the sausage over high heat, stirring, until just cooked through, about 6 minutes.

Place the dough on a pizza paddle that's been dusted with semolina and stretch it to about 12 inches. Spread the pureed tomatoes evenly over the dough. Sprinkle with Pecorino Romano to cover, then scatter the sausage over the top.

Use the paddle to transfer the pie to the pizza stone or steel on the floor of your oven. Bake for 6 to 8 minutes, until the crust is evenly brown and crisp and the cheese begins to brown slightly.

Remove from the oven and dollop ricotta evenly over the cooked pie. Scatter with the arugula and drizzle with EVOO before slicing and serving.

CHERRY JONES

Makes one 12-inch pie

MG: One of our pizza makers, Adam Jones, came up with this one. So Paulie named it after Adam. He just combined Adam's last name with the fact that the pizza had cherries on top, but realized the name sounded familiar. In fact, he thought it sounded like a porn star.

Not being one to watch porn, Paulie had to figure out where he'd heard the name. He did an internet search and realized that Cherry Jones was a well-known actress—and not the adult-film type.

PG: Over the years, a few people have told us that they knew the actress and were going to bring her into the restaurant, but tawk is cheap. The invitation stands, Cherry Jones.

1 round NY-Style Dough (page 22) or your favorite pizza dough (about ½ pound)

Semolina, for dusting

5 ounces shredded low-moisture mozzarella cheese

1 ounce Gorgonzola cheese, crumbled

⅓ cup tart dried cherries

Orange blossom honey, for drizzling

6 thin slices prosciutto

Place a pizza stone or steel on the floor of your oven. Preheat the oven to 550°F or as high as it will go for 45 minutes.

Place the dough on a pizza paddle that's been dusted with semolina and stretch it to about 12 inches. Evenly scatter the mozzarella on top, followed by the Gorgonzola and cherries.

Use the paddle to transfer the pie to the pizza stone or steel on the floor of your oven. Bake for 6 to 8 minutes, until the crust is evenly brown and crisp and the cheese begins to brown slightly.

Remove from the oven and drizzle with honey before slicing into 6 pieces, then place a piece of prosciutto on top of each slice and serve.

BENNY GEE

Makes one 12-inch pie

PG: This dates back to an ill-fated brunch idea in the spring of 2011. We tried to do an eggs Benedict pie with an egg cracked directly on top. But in order for the egg to not overcook, we had to lower the oven temperature a couple hundred degrees. Unacceptable.

MG: That said, it was a delicious pie even without the egg, so we brought it back for nighttime service. When our grandson was born, he was named Benjamin Paul Giannone after Paulie's dad. The Benny Gee is an homage to both of them.

- -

For the Hollandaise Sauce

4 tablespoons (½ stick) unsalted butter

2 large egg yolks

1 tablespoon fresh lemon juice

¼ teaspoon fine sea salt

For the Pizza

1 round NY-Style Dough (page 22) or your favorite pizza dough (about ½ pound)

Semolina, for dusting

5 ounces shredded low-moisture mozzarella cheese

Handful of baby spinach leaves

Olive oil (extra-virgin not necessary), for drizzling

6 thin slices Canadian bacon

NOTE

Leftover hollandaise can't be stored for later. So if you have extra, the obvious answer here is to make more pizzas (like the Greenpoint Florentine, page 70). Which is always the right answer, anyway. Or you can drizzle it on top of asparagus as a side dish.

Place a pizza stone or steel on the floor of your oven. Preheat the oven to 550°F or as high as it will go for 45 minutes.

Make the hollandaise sauce: In a small saucepan, melt the butter over low heat, then remove from the heat and let cool. Combine the egg yolks and lemon juice in a blender and blend on high. While blending, slowly add the melted butter and blend until emulsified, then add the salt and blend briefly to incorporate. Use immediately.

Make the pizza: Place the dough on a pizza paddle that's been dusted with semolina and stretch it to about 12 inches. Scatter the mozzarella over the dough. Toss the spinach leaves with a drizzle of olive oil and scatter them over the mozzarella, then evenly space the Canadian bacon slices on top of the spinach.

Use the paddle to transfer the pie to the pizza stone or steel on the floor of your oven. Bake for 6 to 8 minutes, until the crust is evenly brown and crisp and the cheese begins to brown slightly.

Remove from the oven and drizzle ½ cup of the hollandaise sauce over the top. Cut into 6 slices and serve.

NEFFY'S PORKPIE WHITE

Makes one 12-inch pie

MG: Neftaly Ramirez was one of our favorite staff members. Tragically, Neffy passed away after a bike accident in the neighborhood. We decided to honor him by renaming one of our pizzas Neffy's Porkpie White. We're still in close touch with Neffy's family, who visit 60 Greenpoint frequently.

PG: Porkpie White . . . doesn't it sound like a jazz musician? Two kinds of pork, no tomato sauce.

• •

⅓ cup crumbled sweet Italian fennel sausage (about 1 link, casing removed)

1 round NY-Style Dough (page 22) or your favorite pizza dough (about ½ pound)

Semolina, for dusting

6 ounces shredded low-moisture mozzarella cheese, shredded

7 thin slices soppressata piccante

5 fresh basil leaves

Olive oil (extra-virgin not necessary), for drizzling

Whole-milk ricotta cheese, for dolloping

Hot honey, for drizzling (we use Mike's)

Place a pizza stone or steel on the floor of your oven. Preheat the oven to 550°F or as high as it will go for 45 minutes.

Heat a medium skillet over high heat. Add the sausage and cook, stirring, until just cooked through, about 6 minutes.

Place the dough on a pizza paddle that's been dusted with semolina and stretch it to about 12 inches. Evenly scatter the mozzarella over the top, then space the slices of soppressata evenly around the pie. Do the same with the sausage. Toss the basil leaves with a drizzle of olive oil and evenly space them over the pie.

Use the paddle to transfer the pie to the pizza stone or steel on the floor of your oven. Bake for 6 to 8 minutes, until the crust is evenly brown and crisp and the cheese begins to brown slightly.

Remove from the oven and dollop ricotta over the pie. Drizzle with hot honey before slicing and serving.

MARCELLA MATRICIANA

Makes one 12-inch pie

I created a version of amatriciana sauce shortly after we got married. I used bacon instead of the traditional guanciale because I liked how its smokiness complemented the sweetness of the onion.

Eventually, I got my hands on Marcella Hazan's famous *The Classic Italian Cookbook*, and I found a recipe in there called Tomato Sauce III. It's a very simple sauce that calls for a whole stick of butter as well as a halved onion . . . Then I had this harebrained scheme to put strips of bacon in the sauce as well, so it would have the same flavor as my amatriciana sauce, but a smoother texture.

I went ahead and put it on a pie and really liked it. I named it the Marcella Matriciana, which had a wonderful ring to it. The only problem was, nobody in the restaurant could say it! So I held a contest to come up with a different name.

A regular came up with "Feel Like Bacon Love." We renamed the pie, but since the bacon is used only for flavoring the sauce, we were repeatedly asked, "Where's the bacon?" So I thought, to heck with it, we have to change the name back, and people will learn to pronounce it. And they have. —PG

∎ ∎

For the Bacon-Butter Sauce

2 quarts fresh tomatoes, peeled, or 2 (28-ounce) cans whole peeled Italian-style tomatoes, drained

1 large Vidalia onion, thickly sliced into half-moons

⅔ pound smoked bacon, sliced crosswise into thick strips

1 cup (2 sticks) salted butter

Make the sauce: In a blender, puree the tomatoes until smooth, about 30 seconds, then transfer to a medium saucepan and bring to a gentle boil over medium heat. Reduce the heat to maintain a simmer and add the onion, bacon, and butter. Stir gently so as not to break apart the onion. Simmer, stirring occasionally, until the sauce thickens, about 35 minutes. Using tongs, carefully remove the onion and bacon and discard. If not using the sauce immediately, let it cool, then store in airtight containers in the fridge for up to 5 days or in the freezer indefinitely (see Note).

Make the pizza: Place a pizza stone or steel on the floor of your oven. Preheat the oven to 550°F or as high as it will go for 45 minutes.

Place the dough on a pizza paddle that's been dusted with semolina and stretch it to about 12 inches. Spread ½ cup of the bacon-butter sauce evenly over the dough. Evenly scatter the mozzarella on top.

For the Pizza

1 round NY-Style Dough (page 22) or your favorite pizza dough (about ½ pound)

Semolina, for dusting

4 ounces shredded low-moisture mozzarella cheese

Freshly ground black pepper

Use the paddle to transfer the pie to the pizza stone or steel on the floor of your oven. Bake for 6 to 8 minutes, until the crust is evenly brown and crisp and the cheese begins to brown slightly.

Remove from the oven and grind some pepper over the top before slicing and serving.

NOTE

You can use the leftover sauce for multiple pies or as a topping for pasta. I especially like it with perciatelli or rigatoni.

HELLBOY

Makes one 12-inch pie

In the spring of 2010, Mike Kurtz came into our original location and asked to work as an apprentice making pizza. After arrangements were made, Mike mentioned that he was going to bring his own special condiment when he came in for training. I quickly realized that his goal was as much to get his hot honey on our pies as it was to learn how to make pizza!

I figured that adding it to our Delboy pizza with hot soppressata would really work well. And my instincts were correct. The Hellboy became an immediate sensation. In fact, we eventually trademarked the name. Guests can't get enough of it, and it's still one of our bestsellers. —PG

∎∎∎

1 round NY-Style Dough (page 22) or your favorite pizza dough (about ½ pound)

Semolina, for dusting

¾ cup pureed peeled fresh tomatoes or canned whole peeled Italian-style tomatoes

3 ounces shredded low-moisture mozzarella cheese

Shredded Parmigiano Reggiano cheese

16 slices soppressata piccante

Mike's Hot Honey, for drizzling

Place a pizza stone or steel on the floor of your oven. Preheat the oven to 550°F or as high as it will go for 45 minutes.

Place the dough on a pizza paddle that's been dusted with semolina and stretch it to about 12 inches. Spread the pureed tomatoes evenly over the dough. Evenly scatter the mozzarella on top, then sprinkle with Parmigiano to cover. Space the soppressata slices evenly over the pie.

Use the paddle to transfer the pie to the pizza stone or steel on the floor of your oven. Bake for 6 to 8 minutes, until the crust is evenly brown and crisp and the cheese begins to brown slightly.

Remove from the oven and drizzle with hot honey before slicing and serving.

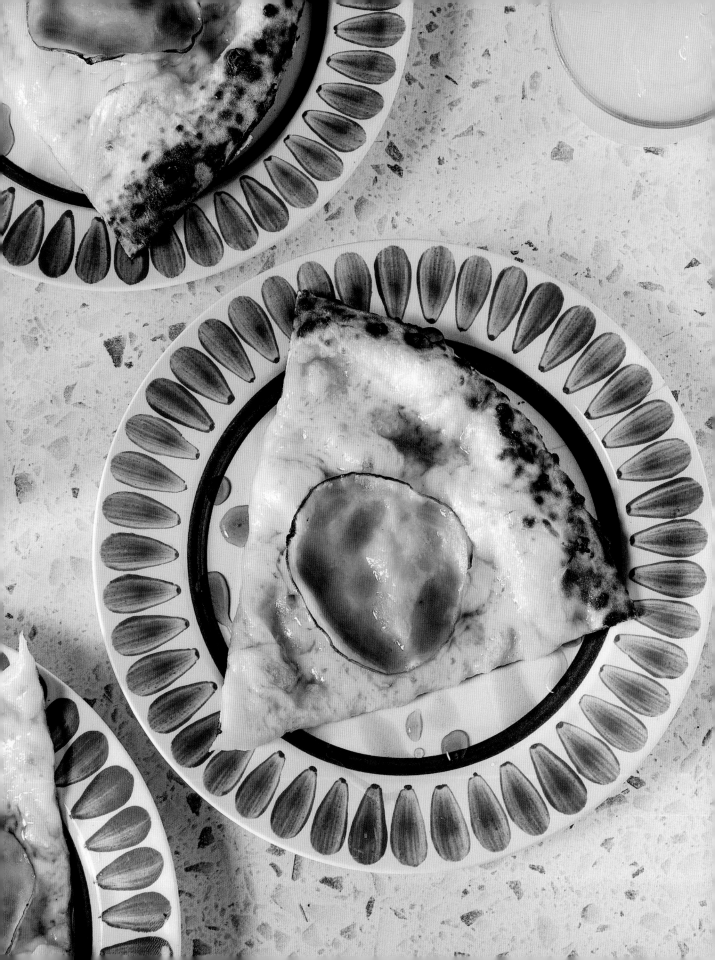

MONTE CRISTO

This was a brunch experiment that made the nighttime menu. Like the sandwich of the same name, it strikes the perfect balance of sweet and savory, and like most brunch items, people tend to enjoy it any time of day. Our hunch was right on keeping it around . . . it's become a real fan favorite. —MG

Makes one 12-inch pie

1 round NY-Style Dough (page 22) or your favorite pizza dough (about ½ pound)

Semolina, for dusting

⅔ cup shredded Gouda cheese

6 thin slices Canadian bacon

Pure maple syrup, for drizzling

Place a pizza stone or steel on the floor of your oven. Preheat the oven to 550°F or as high as it will go for 45 minutes.

Place the dough on a pizza paddle that's been dusted with semolina and stretch it to about 12 inches. Scatter the Gouda over the dough, then space the Canadian bacon slices evenly over the pie.

Use the paddle to transfer the pie to the pizza stone or steel on the floor of your oven. Bake for 6 to 8 minutes, until the crust is evenly brown and crisp and the cheese begins to brown slightly.

Remove from the oven and drizzle maple syrup over the top before slicing and serving.

KING HARRY CLASSIC

Makes one 12-inch pie

There will always be a pie on the menu in memory of our friend Harry Glenn, who was on the ninety-seventh floor of 1 World Trade Center on September 11, 2001. Harry was a king of a man. And we think he'd appreciate this top-quality, universally beloved combo of prosciutto, basil, and Italian tomatoes. Like Harry, it'll never go out of style. —MG

· ·

1 round NY-Style Dough (page 22) or your favorite pizza dough (about ½ pound)

Semolina, for dusting

⅔ cup pureed peeled fresh tomatoes or canned whole peeled Italian-style tomatoes

3 ounces shredded low-moisture mozzarella cheese

5 fresh basil leaves

Olive oil (extra-virgin not necessary), for drizzling

6 thin slices prosciutto

Place a pizza stone or steel on the floor of your oven. Preheat the oven to 550°F or as high as it will go for 45 minutes.

Place the dough on a pizza paddle that's been dusted with semolina and stretch it to about 12 inches. Spread the pureed tomatoes evenly over the dough. Evenly scatter the mozzarella on top. Toss the basil leaves with a drizzle of olive oil and evenly space them over the mozzarella.

Use the paddle to transfer the pie to the pizza stone or steel on the oven floor. Bake for 6 to 8 minutes, until the crust is evenly brown and crisp and the cheese begins to brown slightly.

Remove from the oven and cut into 6 slices, then top each slice with a piece of prosciutto before serving.

HOMETOWN BRISKET

Makes one 12-inch pie

Paulie was looking to furnish one of our franchises, and someone sent us a picture of the chairs at Hometown Bar-B-Que in Red Hook, Brooklyn. Paulie, being Paulie, drove straight to Red Hook, introduced himself to the owner, Billy Durney, and asked where he got his chairs. Of course, Paulie ended up tasting some of the barbecue, too, and Hometown's chopped brisket and BBQ sauce become the centerpiece of this pie. —MG

- -

For the Pickled Red Onions

2 large red onions

2¼ teaspoons whole black peppercorns

3 garlic cloves, peeled

1 cup plus 2 tablespoons red wine vinegar

½ cup plus 1 tablespoon sugar

¾ teaspoon fine sea salt

1½ teaspoons red pepper flakes

For the Pizza

1 round NY-Style Dough (page 22) or your favorite pizza dough (about ½ pound)

Semolina, for dusting

6 ounces shredded low-moisture mozzarella cheese

1 cup barbecued brisket (see Note)

Barbecue sauce, for drizzling

NOTE

You don't need to make an entire brisket for this recipe, although congratulations if you do. This is a good opportunity to support your own local barbecue joint, or use a bit of whatever leftover meat you have around.

Make the pickled red onions: Slice the onions as thinly as you can into rings. Separate all the rings and remove the core pieces. Put the onion rings in a large nonreactive container.

Place the peppercorns and garlic cloves in a piece of cheesecloth and tie it closed with butcher's twine. (A perforated stainless-steel tea holder or really any food-grade item that will keep the peppercorns and garlic contained would also work.)

In a medium saucepan, combine the vinegar, sugar, salt, and red pepper flakes with 1 cup plus 2 tablespoons water and heat over high heat, stirring, until the salt and sugar have completely dissolved. Add the sachet of peppercorns and garlic and bring to a boil, then reduce the heat to low and simmer for 5 minutes.

Pour the mixture over the onions. They should be completely submerged. Place paper towels on top so that no onions are exposed to the air and let sit for several hours before using, or store in an airtight container in the fridge for up to 1 month.

Make the pizza: Place a pizza stone or steel on the floor of your oven. Preheat the oven to 550°F or as high as it will go for 45 minutes.

Place the dough on a pizza paddle dusted with semolina and stretch it to about 12 inches. Scatter the mozzarella evenly over the dough, followed by the brisket.

Use the paddle to transfer the pie to the pizza stone or steel on the floor of your oven. Bake for 6 to 8 minutes, until the crust is evenly brown and crisp and the cheese begins to brown slightly. Remove from the oven and drizzle with barbecue sauce. Scatter with ½ cup of the pickled onions, slice, and serve.

BRISKET FIVE-0

Makes one 12-inch pie

Hometown's brisket is too good for just one pie. We'd been playing around with the idea of adding pickled pineapple into the mix, and beef and pineapple is a great combination. The *Hawaii Five-0* reference seemed obvious, and you better believe the theme song is on Paulie's playlist. —MG

For the Pickled Pineapple

⅓ cup distilled white vinegar

2 tablespoons plus 2 teaspoons apple cider vinegar

2 whole cloves

⅔ cup sugar

1 small cinnamon stick

1 teaspoon fine sea salt

1 fresh pineapple, peeled, cored, and cut into ½-inch pieces

For the Pizza

1 round NY-Style Dough (page 22) or your favorite pizza dough (about ½ pound)

Semolina, for dusting

3 ounces shredded low-moisture mozzarella cheese

1 cup barbecued brisket (see Note, page 46)

⅔ cup shredded Gouda cheese

Make the pickled pineapple: In a large saucepan, combine the white vinegar, apple cider vinegar, cloves, sugar, cinnamon stick, salt, and ½ cup water. Cook over medium heat, stirring occasionally, for 10 minutes. Be careful not to let the mixture boil. Add the pineapple, bring to a rolling boil, and boil for a few seconds. Remove from the heat and let cool before using or storing. Store in airtight containers in the fridge for up to 1 month.

Make the pizza: Place a pizza stone or steel on the floor of your oven. Preheat the oven to 550°F or as high as it will go for 45 minutes.

Place the dough on a pizza paddle that's been dusted with semolina and stretch it to about 12 inches. Evenly top with the mozzarella, followed by the brisket, then the Gouda, then ½ cup of the pickled pineapple.

Use the paddle to transfer the pie to the pizza stone or steel on the floor of your oven. Bake for 6 to 8 minutes, until the crust is evenly brown and crisp and the cheese begins to brown slightly. Slice and serve.

NOTE

Anything pickled is great for keeping around. And unlike the onions on page 46—unless you have unusual tastes—pickled pineapple can be used for either sweet or savory purposes. Tacos, yes, more pizzas, obviously. But also ice cream sundaes, cocktails . . . the list goes on and on.

BETTER OFF FED

Makes one 12-inch pie

My favorite Philly sandwich isn't the cheesesteak. It's the roast pork Italian, with provolone, broccoli rabe, hot cherry peppers . . . the works. So when a Philly-style sandwich shop called Federoff's opened in Brooklyn, I approached the owners about using their roast pork on a pie. They were all for the idea, and not only is this absolutely delicious, it's by far the most attractive pie on the menu. —PG

- -

For the Broccoli Rabe Pesto

1 bunch broccoli rabe

3 garlic cloves, peeled

½ teaspoon red pepper flakes, or more to taste

½ teaspoon fine sea salt, or more to taste

1 cup olive oil, or as needed

For the Pizza

1 round NY-Style Dough (page 22) or your favorite pizza dough (about ½ pound)

Semolina, for dusting

⅔ cup shredded provolone cheese

1 cup shredded Italian roast pork (from your favorite local spot, or use any kind of leftover pork)

½ cup sliced marinated cherry peppers

NOTE

Pesto freezes well and goes with everything, so you never want to make just a little bit.

Make the pesto: Bring a large, high-sided pan of water to a boil over high heat. Fill a bowl with ice and water and set it nearby. Add the broccoli rabe to the boiling water and blanch for about 60 seconds, until it turns bright green. Use tongs or a slotted spoon to immediately transfer it to the bowl of ice water to stop the cooking process. Drain, then coarsely chop. Make sure to squeeze the water out of the broccoli rabe, then transfer it to a food processor.

Add the garlic, red pepper flakes, and salt, then turn on the processor and slowly stream in the olive oil until the pesto achieves a thick, saucy consistency. (You may need more or less oil; just go slowly and keep your eye on things.) Adjust the seasonings to taste.

Make the pizza: Place a pizza stone or steel on the floor of your oven. Preheat the oven to 550°F or as high as it will go for 45 minutes.

Place the dough on a pizza paddle that's been dusted with semolina and stretch it to about 12 inches. Evenly scatter the provolone over the top, followed by the roast pork. Space 6 dollops of the broccoli rabe pesto over the pie. (Store any extra pesto in an airtight container in the fridge, with a piece of plastic wrap placed directly on top of the pesto so it doesn't turn brown, for up to 5 days; see Note). Scatter the pie with the cherry peppers.

Use the paddle to transfer the pie to the pizza stone or steel on the floor of your oven. Bake for 6 to 8 minutes, until the crust is evenly brown and crisp and the cheese begins to brown slightly. Slice and serve.

SPECTACLE 261 & SPECTACLE TOO

Makes one 12-inch pie

Roberta's in Brooklyn is one of my greatest influences. And my favorite pie of theirs is the Speckenwolf, with red onion and speck.

I wanted to steal that pie, in a way that honored them, of course, so I made a few Paulie Gee changes to the recipe. And since I didn't want to steal the name as well as the pie, I decided to call it the Spectacle 261, after their location on 261 Moore Street.

The Spectacle Too is a variation that includes pureed tomatoes. I thought that sounded better than the Spectacle Also. —**PG**

1 round NY-Style Dough (page 22) or your favorite pizza dough (about ½ pound)

Semolina, for dusting

⅔ cup pureed peeled fresh tomatoes or canned whole peeled Italian-style tomatoes (optional)

3 ounces shredded low-moisture mozzarella cheese

1 cup sliced cremini mushrooms

6 thin slices speck

Place a pizza stone or steel on the floor of your oven. Preheat the oven to 550°F or as high as it will go for 45 minutes.

Place the dough on a pizza paddle that's been dusted with semolina and stretch it to about 12 inches. If making the Spectacle Too, spread the pureed tomatoes evenly over the dough. For either pie, scatter the mozzarella on top, followed by the mushrooms.

Use the paddle to transfer the pie to the pizza stone or steel on the oven floor. Bake for 6 to 8 minutes, until the crust is evenly brown and crisp and the cheese begins to brown slightly.

Remove from the oven and cut into 6 slices, then top each slice with a piece of speck before serving.

XI'AN FAMOUS PIZZA

Makes one 12-inch pie

Years ago, after trying Xi'an Famous Foods's housemade chili oil and chili crisp (an absolute umami bomb of dried chiles, fried garlic, and spicy infused oil), Paulie knew he had to put it on a pie. We don't recall the name of that pie or what else we put on it at that time, but it was pretty popular . . . well, until we were told by Xi'an that they could no longer supply us with their spicy oil.

In 2022, Xi'an Famous Foods owner Jason Wang reached out to let us know that they were once again officially selling their chili crisp, and he thought it would be a great collaboration with us to include it on a pie. He had no memory of the original pie, or of cutting off the supply of oil in the first place, but the Xi'an Famous Pizza 2.0 is better than ever, especially since it now includes a topping of chili crisp and ground lamb. —MG

¾ cup ground lamb

1 round NY-Style Dough (page 22) or your favorite pizza dough (about ½ pound)

Semolina, for dusting

2 cups baby spinach

4 heaping tablespoons Chinese chili crisp

3 tablespoons olive oil

Place a pizza stone or steel on the floor of your oven. Preheat the oven to 550°F or as high as it will go for 45 minutes.

In a medium skillet, cook the lamb over high heat, stirring, until just cooked through, about 1 minute.

Place the dough on a pizza paddle that's been dusted with semolina and stretch to about 12 inches. Scatter the spinach evenly over the dough, followed by the cooked lamb. Drizzle with the chili crisp, followed by the olive oil.

Use the paddle to transfer the pie to the pizza stone or steel on the oven floor. Bake for 6 to 8 minutes, until the crust is evenly brown and crisp. Remove from the oven, slice, and serve.

NOTE

To make this vegan, simply swap in 1½ cups chopped Vegan Sausage (see page 102) for the ground lamb.

MO CHEEKS

Makes one 12-inch pie

Paulie loves guanciale, a cured meat made from pork cheeks. And Mo Cheeks is one of his favorite basketball players. One night, a customer asked Paulie how he came up with the name of this pie. His response: "Why do you want to know? Is he your father or something?" Well, the answer was yes. His coworkers had told him there was a Greenpoint pizzeria with a pie named after his dad, and he just had to come in and find out why. He's been a patron ever since. —MG

∙∙

1 round NY-Style Dough (page 22) or your favorite pizza dough (about ½ pound)

Semolina, for dusting

¾ cup pureed peeled fresh tomatoes or canned whole peeled Italian-style tomatoes

Small handful of shaved Pecorino Romano cheese

6 slices guanciale

Grated Parmigiano Reggiano cheese, for sprinkling

½ cup Pickled Red Onions (see page 46)

Place a pizza stone or steel on the floor of your oven. Preheat the oven to 550°F or as high as it will go for 45 minutes.

Place the dough on a pizza paddle that's been dusted with semolina and stretch it to about 12 inches. Spread the pureed tomatoes evenly over the dough. Scatter the pecorino over the top, then evenly space the guanciale slices over that. Sprinkle with Parmigiano.

Use the paddle to transfer the pie to the pizza stone or steel on the oven floor. Bake for 6 to 8 minutes, until the crust is evenly brown and crisp and the cheese begins to brown slightly.

Remove from the oven and scatter the pickled onions over the top before slicing and serving.

ANISE & ANEPHEW

Makes one 12-inch pie

We were at dinner with friends one night prior to the restaurant opening, and someone ordered swordfish with an anisette cream sauce. Paulie's mind immediately went to how he could combine that sweet sauce with something savory on a pie. He'd recently discovered guanciale and decided to try it with the sauce. It turned out to be the perfect combo, along with braised fennel slices and fresh fennel fronds.

Paulie had been looking to dedicate a pie to our nephew Justin—who'd been very helpful at coming up with the restaurant design and logo—as well as his twin sister, Diane. Paulie often referred to the two of them as "Denise and Denephew." Thus the name. —MG

. . . .

For the Anisette Cream

¼ cup anisette liqueur

1 cup heavy cream

For the Braised Fennel

1 fennel bulb with fronds

Olive oil (extra-virgin not necessary)

Vegetable broth

For the Pizza

1 round NY-Style Dough (page 22) or your favorite pizza dough (about ½ pound)

Semolina, for dusting

6 ounces shredded low-moisture mozzarella cheese

6 thin slices guanciale

Make the anisette cream: In a high-sided medium pot, combine the liqueur and cream. (Keep in mind that when heated, the mixture will foam up 6 inches, so the pot needs to be tall enough to contain this.) Cook over high heat, whisking continuously and paying attention to the cream, until the cream thickens (but doesn't become so thick that it can't be easily applied to a pizza through a squeeze bottle), about 15 minutes. Allow the cream to boil up to the rim of the pot without spilling over, then let the cream reduce by about half. It will start to look yellowish. Remove from the heat and let cool completely before using.

Make the braised fennel: Chop off the bottom and stalks of the fennel bulb. Save the fronds for garnish. Quarter the bulb from top to bottom, then separate the layers and slice each quarter into thin strips (like french fries; about ½ inch wide). Place the strips in a colander and rinse them with cold water. Dry well.

In a medium pan, heat a splash of olive oil over medium-high heat for a few seconds, then add the fennel. Cook, stirring, until golden brown and caramelized, about 5 minutes.

Reduce the heat slightly and add a splash of broth, enough to coat all the fennel strips evenly. Cook until the fennel is soft, about 8 minutes more. Remove from the heat and let the braised fennel cool before using.

A clear use for leftover anisette cream is to drizzle it over grilled swordfish, the vehicle for which it was originally intended.

Make the pizza: Place a pizza stone or steel on the floor of your oven. Preheat the oven to 550°F or as high as it will go for 45 minutes.

Place the dough on a pizza paddle that's been dusted with semolina and stretch it to about 12 inches. Scatter the mozzarella evenly over the pie, then top with 6 dollops of the anisette cream. Evenly place the braised fennel over that, followed by the guanciale.

Use the paddle to transfer the pie to the pizza stone or steel on the oven floor. Bake for 6 to 8 minutes, until the crust is evenly brown and crisp and the cheese begins to brown slightly.

Remove from the oven and top with the reserved fennel fronds before slicing and serving.

JIMMY PARMODY

Makes one 12-inch pie

If you watched *Boardwalk Empire* on HBO, you'll recognize "Jimmy Parmody" as a play on the character named Jimmy Darmody. We were further inspired by the fact that there was a mockup of the boardwalk at the far northern end of Greenpoint, and they likely filmed some of Jimmy's scenes right in our own backyard. The show may not be on the air anymore, but the pizza isn't coming off our menu anytime soon. **—PG**

1 round NY-Style Dough (page 22) or your favorite pizza dough (about ½ pound)

Semolina, for dusting

⅔ cup shaved Parmigiano Reggiano cheese

½ small red onion, thinly sliced

12 thin slices soppressata piccante

Place a pizza stone or steel on the floor of your oven. Preheat the oven to 550°F or as high as it will go for 45 minutes.

Place the dough on a pizza paddle that's been dusted with semolina and stretch it to about 12 inches. Scatter the Parmigiano evenly over the dough, followed by the onion and soppressata.

Use the paddle to transfer the pie to the pizza stone or steel on the oven floor. Bake for 6 to 8 minutes, until the crust is evenly brown and crisp and the cheese begins to brown slightly. Slice and serve.

RED, WHITE & GREENBERG

Makes one 12-inch pie

Our kitchen manager and pizza maker, Jon Greenberg, suggested we make a white pie with pancetta and pickled red onions. Paulie decided to go with guanciale instead of pancetta, but still wanted to name it after Jonny. He thought to call it the Red, White & Greenberg. Only problem was, nothing about it was green. Hence the addition of arugula. —MG

- -

1 round NY-Style Dough (page 22) or your favorite pizza dough (about ½ pound)

Semolina, for dusting

6 ounces shredded low-moisture mozzarella cheese

Generous handful of baby arugula

Olive oil (extra-virgin not necessary), for drizzling

6 thin slices guanciale

½ cup Pickled Red Onions (see page 46)

Place a pizza stone or steel on the floor of your oven. Preheat the oven to 550°F or as high as it will go for 45 minutes.

Place the dough on a pizza paddle that's been dusted with semolina and stretch it to about 12 inches. Scatter the mozzarella evenly over the dough. Toss the arugula with a drizzle of olive oil and evenly scatter it across the pie. Evenly space the guanciale over the top.

Use the paddle to transfer the pie to the pizza stone or steel on the oven floor. Bake for 6 to 8 minutes, until the crust is evenly brown and crisp and the cheese begins to brown slightly.

Remove from the oven and top with the pickled onions before slicing and serving.

CHAPTER TWO

BETTER OFF VEG

"There are no bests, only favorites."

Balance is key for all our pies, but that means something different depending on which kind of pie you're talking about. In the meat-topped pies, balance refers more to how the sweet and savory flavors play against each other. With vegetarian, it's all about an optimal bite ratio. Just the right amount of this and just the right amount of that, with no single ingredient overtaking the other.

Another thing that sets our vegetarian pies apart is that we don't just throw a bunch of vegetables on top of them and call it a day. As much TLC goes into their construction as any of our other pies, which includes a commitment to quality and making a lot of the ingredients ourselves. **—PG**

Paulie's Playlist

"Rocky Mountain Way," Joe Walsh

"A Whiter Shade of Pale," Procol Harum

"Mama Tried," Grateful Dead

"Someday We'll All Be Free," Donny Hathaway

"Riders on the Storm," The Doors

"From the Beginning," Emerson, Lake & Palmer

"Stars Fell on Alabama," Frank Sinatra

THE GREEN-POINTER

Makes one 12-inch pie

This is one of the favorite combos we came up with while experimenting in our suburban wood-burning oven. So it only made sense for it to become one of our first official Paulie Gee's pies, named after the neighborhood where we began our business and that became our second home.

It wasn't until later that Paulie realized he'd taken the entire idea for this pie from Roberta's own Green & White. So thank you to the entire team at Roberta's! —MG

- -

1 round NY-Style Dough (page 22) or your favorite pizza dough (about ½ pound)

Semolina, for dusting

6 ounces shredded low-moisture mozzarella cheese

Handful of arugula

Extra-virgin olive oil, for drizzling

Juice of ½ lemon

Fine sea salt (optional)

¼ cup shaved Parmigiano Reggiano cheese

Place a pizza stone or steel on the floor of your oven. Preheat the oven to 550°F or as high as it will go for 45 minutes.

Place the dough on a pizza paddle that's been dusted with semolina and stretch it to about 12 inches. Evenly scatter the mozzarella on top of the dough.

Use the paddle to transfer the pie to the pizza stone or steel on the oven floor. Bake for 6 to 8 minutes, until the crust is evenly brown and crisp and the cheese begins to brown slightly.

Remove from the oven and evenly scatter the arugula over the pie. Drizzle with EVOO and the lemon juice and sprinkle with a bit of salt to taste, if desired. Top with the Parmigiano before slicing and serving.

NOTE

Simply substitute your favorite vegan cheeses for the mozz and Parmigiano for a vegan version.

GREENPOINT FLORENTINE

If you're going to have brunch for dinner (and don't do meat), this is way better than avocado toast. —MG

Makes one 12-inch pie

....

1 round NY-Style Dough (page 22) or your favorite pizza dough (about ½ pound)

Semolina, for dusting

6 ounces shredded low-moisture mozzarella cheese

2 cups baby spinach leaves

Olive oil (extra-virgin not necessary), for drizzling

1 cup sliced cremini mushrooms

Hollandaise Sauce (see page 34)

Place a pizza stone or steel on the floor of your oven. Preheat the oven to 550°F or as high as it will go for 45 minutes.

Place the dough on a pizza paddle that's been dusted with semolina and stretch it to about 12 inches. Evenly scatter the mozzarella over the dough. Toss the spinach leaves with a drizzle of olive oil and evenly space them over the pie, followed by the mushrooms.

Use the paddle to transfer the pie to the pizza stone or steel on the oven floor. Bake for 6 to 8 minutes, until the crust is evenly brown and crisp and the cheese begins to brown slightly.

Remove from the oven and top with a generous drizzle of hollandaise before slicing and serving.

SAKE MOUNTAIN WAY

Makes one 12-inch pie

We'd purchased a whole case of sake once for brunch service in order to make Bloody Samurais, since we only had a beer-and-wine license at the time. When we decided to discontinue brunch, we didn't want the sake to go to waste. Paulie started making pasta with sake sauce instead of vodka sauce for staff meals, and he found that it added extra umami. As always, the discovery found its way onto pizza. —MG

- -

For the Sake Pink Sauce

1 cup sake

2 cups Vegan Tomato Sauce (see page 91) or your favorite tomato sauce

¼ cup heavy cream

For the Pizza

1 round NY-Style Dough (page 22) or your favorite pizza dough (about ½ pound)

Semolina, for dusting

3 ounces shredded low-moisture mozzarella cheese

NOTE

Any leftover sauce is delicious over pasta or used as a dip for our Garlic Bread (page 197).

Make the sauce: In a medium saucepan, combine the sake and tomato sauce and cook over medium-high heat, stirring frequently, for 12 minutes to allow the alcohol to cook off and thicken the sauce slightly. Remove from the heat; stir in the heavy cream just before using.

Make the pizza: Place a pizza stone or steel on the floor of your oven. Preheat the oven to 550°F or as high as it will go for 45 minutes.

Place the dough on a pizza paddle that's been dusted with semolina and stretch it to about 12 inches. Evenly spread 1 cup of the sake pink sauce over the dough and top with the mozzarella.

Use the paddle to transfer the pie to the pizza stone or steel on the oven floor. Bake for 6 to 8 minutes, until the crust is evenly brown and crisp and the cheese begins to brown slightly. Slice and serve.

BETTER OFF VEG

Makes one 12-inch pie

An Italian-roast-pork-inspired pizza without the pork? Believe it. Our homemade broccoli rabe pesto speaks loudly enough to do most of the tawkin'. —PG

■ ■

1 round NY-Style Dough (page 22) or your favorite pizza dough (about ½ pound)

Semolina, for dusting

1 cup shredded provolone cheese

6 dollops of Broccoli Rabe Pesto (see page 51)

½ cup sliced marinated cherry peppers

Place a pizza stone or steel on the floor of your oven. Preheat the oven to 550°F or as high as it will go for 45 minutes.

Place the dough on a pizza paddle that's been dusted with semolina and stretch it to about 12 inches. Top evenly with the provolone, then dollop with the pesto and scatter the cherry peppers over the top.

Use the paddle to transfer the pie to the pizza stone or steel on the oven floor. Bake for 6 to 8 minutes, until the crust is evenly brown and crisp and the cheese begins to brown slightly. Slice and serve.

DANIELA SPINACI

This pie was created by our pizza maker Daniela Bustamante. She was such a focused and enthusiastic member of our pizza-making team, she deserved to be rewarded for her efforts with a namesake pie. —MG

Makes one 12-inch pie

- -

1 round NY-Style Dough (page 22) or your favorite pizza dough (about ½ pound)

Semolina, for dusting

1 teaspoon thinly sliced garlic

6 ounces shredded low-moisture mozzarella cheese

2 cups baby spinach leaves

Olive oil (extra-virgin not necessary), for drizzling

Shaved Parmigiano Reggiano cheese, for sprinkling

Place a pizza stone or steel on the floor of your oven. Preheat the oven to 550°F or as high as it will go for 45 minutes.

Place the dough on a pizza paddle that's been dusted with semolina and stretch it to about 12 inches. Evenly scatter the garlic over the dough, followed by the mozzarella. Toss the spinach leaves with a drizzle of olive oil, then space them evenly over the pie, followed by a generous sprinkle of Parmigiano.

Use the paddle to transfer the pie to the pizza stone or steel on the oven floor. Bake for 6 to 8 minutes, until the crust is evenly brown and crisp and the cheese begins to brown slightly. Slice and serve.

THE MOOTZ

Makes one 12-inch pie

Other not-to-be-named pizzerias would refer to this as the "cheese lover's," but that's clearly not our style. Our son's nickname in high school was Mickey Mootz. And this has got a lot more mootz than most of our other pies. —MG

- -

1 round NY-Style Dough (page 22) or your favorite pizza dough (about ½ pound)

Semolina, for dusting

6 ounces shredded low-moisture mozzarella cheese

1 teaspoon thinly sliced garlic

6 fresh basil leaves

Place a pizza stone or steel on the floor of your oven. Preheat the oven to 550°F or as high as it will go for 45 minutes.

Place the dough on a pizza paddle that's been dusted with semolina and stretch it to about 12 inches. Evenly scatter the mozzarella over the dough, followed by the garlic and the basil leaves.

Use the paddle to transfer the pie to the pizza stone or steel on the oven floor. Bake for 6 to 8 minutes, until the crust is evenly brown and crisp and the cheese begins to brown slightly. Slice and serve.

REGINA

We needed a pie named for Mrs. Gee, my queen. Simple, elegant, perfect. —PG

- -

1 round NY-Style Dough (page 22) or your favorite pizza dough (about ½ pound)

Semolina, for dusting

⅔ cup pureed peeled fresh tomatoes or canned whole peeled Italian-style tomatoes

3 ounces shredded low-moisture mozzarella cheese

6 fresh basil leaves

Place a pizza stone or steel on the floor of your oven. Preheat the oven to 550°F or as high as it will go for 45 minutes.

Place the dough on a pizza paddle that's been dusted with semolina and stretch it to about 12 inches. Evenly spread the pureed tomatoes over the dough. Scatter the mozzarella evenly over the top and finish with the basil leaves.

Use the paddle to transfer the pie to the pizza stone or steel on the oven floor. Bake for 6 to 8 minutes, until the crust is evenly brown and crisp and the cheese begins to brown slightly. Slice and serve.

NOTE

For a vegan version, use vegan cheese in place of the mozz (and, even better, use our Vegan Tomato Sauce, page 91, instead of the pureed tomatoes).

WHITER SHADE OF KALE

Makes one 12-inch pie

When Paulie found out that one of his favorite lyricists—Keith Reid of the band Procol Harum—was coming to the restaurant, he hurried to come up with a pie. He named it Whiter Shade of Kale after Keith's most famous song, but the pie itself didn't stay on the menu for long because we didn't like how charred the fresh kale got in our 900°F oven. Using kale pesto instead allowed us to resurrect the pie . . . and one of our most clever names. And it tastes great, too! —MG

■ ■

For the Vegan Kale Pesto

1 pound baby kale (about 6 cups)

8 medium garlic cloves, peeled

3 tablespoons fresh lemon juice

1 tablespoon plus ¾ teaspoon fine sea salt

1½ teaspoons freshly ground black pepper

1½ tablespoons nutritional yeast

2 cups extra-virgin olive oil

For the Pizza

1 round NY-Style Dough (page 22) or your favorite pizza dough (about ½ pound)

Semolina, for dusting

3 ounces shredded low-moisture mozzarella cheese

Make the vegan kale pesto: In a food processor, combine half the kale, the garlic, lemon juice, salt, pepper, nutritional yeast, and just a drizzle of the olive oil to start. Process for a few seconds, then add the rest of the kale and olive oil. Process until the kale is completely broken down and the pesto is emulsified.

Make the pizza: Place a pizza stone or steel on the floor of your oven. Preheat the oven to 550°F or as high as it will go for 45 minutes.

Place the dough on a pizza paddle that's been dusted with semolina and stretch it to about 12 inches. Spread 1 cup of the kale pesto evenly over the dough, followed by the mozzarella. (Store any unused pesto in an airtight container with a piece of plastic wrap pressed directly against the surface of the pesto to prevent it from browning. It will keep in the fridge for up to 1 week; see Note.)

Use the paddle to transfer the pie to the pizza stone or steel on the oven floor. Bake for 6 to 8 minutes, until the crust is evenly brown and crisp and the cheese begins to brown slightly. Slice and serve.

NOTE

Nothing freezes quite as wonderfully as pesto, which you can store for up to 1 year. You can even freeze it in ice cube trays so you can pop out individual blocks to use as needed for pizzas, pastas, salad dressings, or just about anything else.

BRIAN DEPARMA

Makes one 12-inch pie

■ ■

1 round NY-Style Dough (page 22) or your favorite pizza dough (about ½ pound)

Semolina, for dusting

⅔ cup pureed peeled fresh tomatoes or canned whole peeled Italian-style tomatoes

⅔ cup shaved Parmigiano Reggiano cheese

Grated Parmigiano Reggiano cheese, for sprinkling

Place a pizza stone or steel on the floor of your oven. Preheat the oven to 550°F or as high as it will go for 45 minutes.

Place the dough on a pizza paddle that's been dusted with semolina and stretch it to about 12 inches. Spread the pureed tomatoes evenly over the dough. Evenly scatter the shaved Parmigiano over the top.

Use the paddle to transfer the pie to the pizza stone or steel on the oven floor. Bake for 6 to 8 minutes, until the crust is evenly brown and crisp and the cheese begins to brown slightly.

Remove from the oven and sprinkle some grated Parmigiano over the top. Slice and serve.

NOT THE QUATTRO FORMAGGI

Makes one 12-inch pie

You'll find this four-cheese pie on our secret menu. Secret's out, I guess. I really like this pie but I really hate clichés, so I had to push back on the name. I mean, how many pies out there are called the "Quattro Formaggi"? —PG

■■

1 round NY-Style Dough (page 22) or your favorite pizza dough (about ½ pound)

Semolina, for dusting

3 ounces shredded low-moisture mozzarella cheese

¼ cup shredded Parmigiano Reggiano cheese

¼ cup shredded Pecorino Romano cheese

¼ cup crumbled Gorgonzola cheese

Place a pizza stone or steel on the floor of your oven. Preheat the oven to 550°F or as high as it will go for 45 minutes.

Place the dough on a pizza paddle that's been dusted with semolina and stretch it to about 12 inches. Evenly scatter the mozzarella over the dough, followed by the Parm and pecorino, and then the Gorgonzola.

Use the paddle to transfer the pie to the pizza stone or steel on the oven floor. Bake for 6 to 8 minutes, until the crust is evenly brown and crisp and the cheese begins to brown slightly. Slice and serve.

CHAPTER THREE

IN RICOTTA DA VEGAN

> ## "Walk through the walls of fear. It's paper-thin, and there's only good stuff on the other side."

When we first opened, I realized I had joined a community that contained a lot of vegans. I wanted to be able to serve those people, and I liked the challenge of coming up with a pie that was vegan but actually tasted good. Because, unfortunately, vegans have become accustomed to accepting just about anything, as long as it's labeled "vegan."

At first, I just put a little blurb on the menu that read, *Ask us about our vegan variations.* I liked the sound of that. I thought it was cute. But nobody asked, okay? So I decided we needed to force-feed it a bit by coming up with a separate vegan menu. We started with about six pies.

But I wasn't very satisfied with the vegan ingredients I found on the market. Take, for example, a vegan sausage that was beautifully packaged, but really should have had a horse on the cover—because it tasted like horseshit. I said, "Look, if we're going to do this, we need to start making our own vegan ingredients. If we can make better than what's out there, then we need to do it." We started with vegan sausage and tackled vegan cheese next. I'd actually stopped using vegan cheese completely on our vegan pies, because everything we found tasted like butter or worse. We came up with a cashew ricotta (see page 99), and I actually like it better than real ricotta.

Our Ricotta da Vegan is the vegan version of the Ricky Ricotta, and I'm not a vegan, okay? But to this day, you can put the pies next to each other and I'll choose the Ricotta da Vegan each time. **—PG**

Paulie's Playlist

"In-A-Gadda-Da-Vida," Iron Butterfly

"Peace Train," Cat Stevens

"Green, Green Grass of Home," Tom Jones

"Sussudio," Phil Collins

"Grazing in the Grass," Hugh Masekela

"I Wanna Be Like You," Louie Prima

"Talk to the Animals," Bobby Darin

"I'll Stand by You," The Pretenders

"Meat Is Murder," The Smiths

ARUGULA SHMOOGULA

Makes one 12-inch pie

What makes this sauce vegan? It's the sauce we exclusively use for our vegan pies.

When we first started experimenting with a vegan menu, we found that the pies lacked umami. I didn't like any of the vegan cheeses that were available at the time, and you can only put so much salt on things (preferably none).

In true Neapolitan style, we just use pureed Italian fresh tomatoes on most of our pies. That's it.

But the vegan pies needed a boost, and a cooked sauce with aromatics did the trick. Although thankfully, vegan cheeses have gotten a lot better over the years. —**PG**

For the Vegan Tomato Sauce

2 quarts fresh tomatoes, peeled, or 2 (28-ounce) cans whole peeled Italian-style tomatoes, drained

½ cup olive oil

2 garlic cloves, crushed

½ Vidalia onion, finely diced

For the Aleppo Chile Oil

½ cup olive oil

2¼ teaspoons Aleppo chile flakes or powder

For the Pizza

1 round NY-Style Dough (page 22) or your favorite pizza dough (about ½ pound)

Semolina, for dusting

Shredded vegan Parmesan, for sprinkling

Small handful of baby arugula

Extra-virgin olive oil, for drizzling

NOTE

You'll have leftover sauce here. But why bother making only a little bit of sauce?

Make the tomato sauce: Puree the tomatoes in a blender. Heat the olive oil in a large saucepan over medium heat. Add the garlic and cook, stirring, until fragrant and golden in color, about 1 minute. Remove the garlic with a slotted spoon and discard. Add the onion and cook, stirring, until golden brown, about 3 minutes. Add the pureed tomatoes and bring to a boil, stirring occasionally. Reduce the heat to maintain a simmer and cook, stirring occasionally to prevent burning, for 1 hour. Remove from the heat.

Make the Aleppo chile oil: In a small saucepan, combine the oil and chile flakes. Cook over medium heat, keeping the oil at no higher than a simmer and stirring occasionally so the chile flakes don't burn, for about 7 minutes. Turn off the heat and let cool completely. Strain through a fine-mesh strainer before using.

Make the pizza: Place a pizza stone or steel on the floor of your oven. Preheat the oven to 550°F or as high as it will go for 45 minutes.

Place the dough on a pizza paddle that's been dusted with semolina and stretch it to about 12 inches. Spread two heaping spoonfuls of the tomato sauce evenly over the dough. Sprinkle with the cheese and scatter with the arugula. Evenly drizzle with about 2 tablespoons EVOO.

Use the paddle to transfer the pie to the pizza stone or steel on the oven floor. Bake for 6 to 8 minutes, until the crust is evenly brown and crisp. Drizzle with some Aleppo chile oil before slicing and serving.

VEGAN SPINACI

Makes one 12-inch pie

Any time we make a pie vegan, we look for ways to bump up the umami factor. A drizzle of Aleppo chile oil is perfect. That's why it makes sense to prepare a bunch of it at a time, and keep it on hand for drizzling whenever you're not using dairy or meat. —MG

■ ■

1 round NY-Style Dough (page 22) or your favorite pizza dough (about ½ pound)

Semolina, for dusting

1 teaspoon thinly sliced garlic

1½ cups shredded vegan mozzarella

2 cups baby spinach

Olive oil (extra-virgin not necessary), for drizzling

Shredded vegan Parmesan, for sprinkling

Aleppo Chile Oil (see page 91), for drizzling

Place a pizza stone or steel on the floor of your oven. Preheat the oven to 550°F or as high as it will go for 45 minutes.

Place the dough on a pizza paddle that's been dusted with semolina and stretch it to about 12 inches. Evenly scatter the garlic over the dough, followed by the mozzarella. Toss the spinach leaves with a drizzle of olive oil, then space them evenly over the pie, followed by a generous sprinkle of Parm.

Use the paddle to transfer the pie to the pizza stone or steel on the oven floor. Bake for 6 to 8 minutes, until the crust is evenly brown and crisp and the cheese begins to brown slightly.

Remove from the oven and drizzle some Aleppo chile oil over the top before slicing and serving.

MY, MY, MY VIDALIA

Makes one 12-inch pie

The name was taken from a line in one of my favorite Tom Jones songs, "Delilah." And if you're not aware of the story that's told in this very upbeat-sounding song, please do a search on the lyrics. You'll be surprised. As for the pizza, it's a lot sweeter than the story. Vidalia onions are known for being mild and sweet enough to eat raw, and are even better when cooked. —PG

1 tablespoon olive oil (extra-virgin not necessary)

½ cup thinly sliced Vidalia onion

1 round NY-Style Dough (page 22) or your favorite pizza dough (about ½ pound)

Semolina, for dusting

½ cup Vegan Tomato Sauce (see page 91) or your favorite sauce

¾ cup shredded vegan Parmesan

Place a pizza stone or steel on the floor of your oven. Preheat the oven to 550°F or as high as it will go for 45 minutes.

In a large saucepan, heat the olive oil over medium heat until hot but not smoking. Add the onion, stir to coat with the oil, and reduce the heat to low. Cook, stirring occasionally, until the onions are soft and caramelized, 15 to 20 minutes.

Place the dough on a pizza paddle that's been dusted with semolina and stretch it to about 12 inches. Spread the sauce evenly over the dough. Evenly scatter the Parmesan on top, followed by the caramelized onions.

Use the paddle to transfer the pie to the pizza stone or steel on the oven floor. Bake for 6 to 8 minutes, until the crust is evenly brown and crisp and the cheese begins to brown slightly. Slice and serve.

I GOT THE CHOPT

Makes one 12-inch pie

Both the original and vegan versions of this pie came about as part of a collaboration with the folks at Chopt Creative Salad, who were interested in having us use one of their creations on a pie. We went with their kale pesto, but eventually came up with a nut-free version of our own. Not that we'll ever take credit for the original idea. **—MG**

1 round NY-Style Dough (page 22) or your favorite pizza dough (about ½ pound)

Semolina, for dusting

½ cup Vegan Kale Pesto (see page 80)

½ cup shredded vegan mozzarella

½ cup sliced cremini mushrooms

Place a pizza stone or steel on the floor of your oven. Preheat the oven to 550°F or as high as it will go for 45 minutes.

Place the dough on a pizza paddle that's been dusted with semolina and stretch it to about 12 inches. Spread the kale pesto evenly over the dough. Scatter the mozzarella on top, followed by the mushrooms.

Use the paddle to transfer the pie to the pizza stone or steel on the oven floor. Bake for 6 to 8 minutes, until the crust is evenly brown and crisp and the cheese begins to brown slightly. Slice and serve.

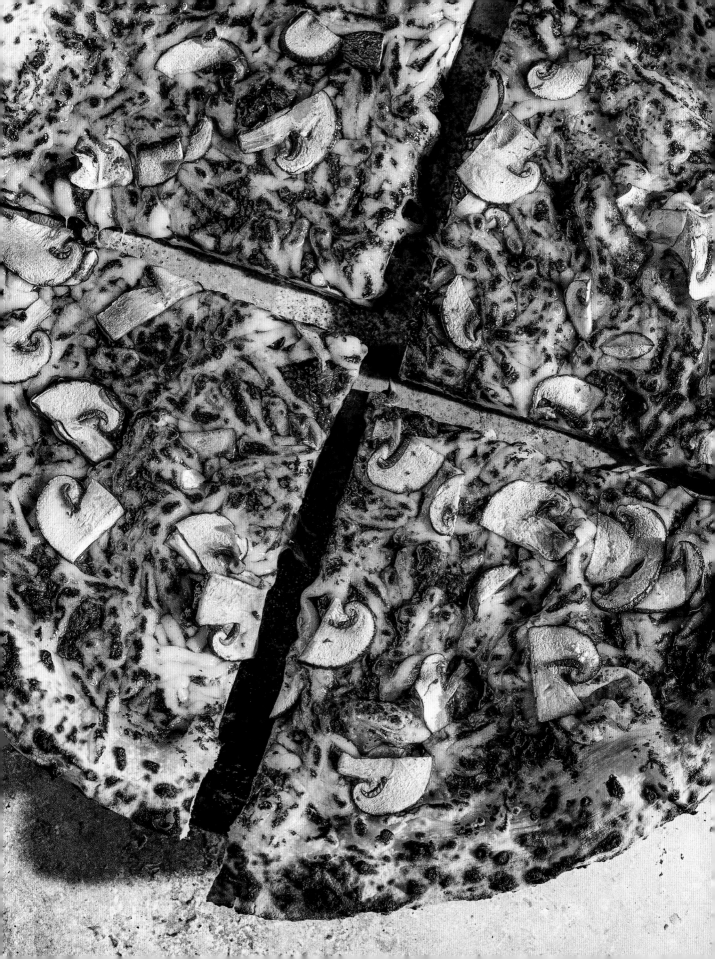

RED, WHITE & GREENPEACE

Makes one 12-inch pie

This riff on the Red, White & Greenberg (page 62) features our famous cashew ricotta, which I prefer to the real thing. I didn't scale back the quantity at all for this recipe, because once you try it, you're going to want to use it on everything. —PG

·····································

For the Cashew Ricotta

1 pound raw cashews (about 3 cups)

1 teaspoon sugar

1¾ teaspoons fresh lemon juice

1½ teaspoons fine sea salt

1½ cups warm water

For the Pizza

1 round NY-Style Dough (page 22) or your favorite pizza dough (about ½ pound)

Semolina, for dusting

2 cups arugula

Olive oil (extra-virgin not necessary), for drizzling

½ cup Pickled Red Onions (see page 46)

Make the cashew ricotta: Place the cashews in a large bowl and add cold water to cover by a few inches. (There should be enough water so that the cashews remain submerged as they expand overnight.) Set aside to soak overnight.

The next day, drain the cashews and transfer them to a blender. Add the sugar, lemon juice, salt, and warm water and blend until smooth. Set a fine-mesh strainer over a large bowl and pour the cashew mixture into the strainer. Set aside to drain for at least 1 hour before using.

Make the pizza: Place a pizza stone or steel on the floor of your oven. Preheat the oven to 550°F or as high as it will go for 45 minutes.

Place the dough on a pizza paddle that's been dusted with semolina and stretch it to about 12 inches. Toss the arugula with a drizzle of olive oil, then space the leaves evenly over the pie.

Use the paddle to transfer the pie to the pizza stone or steel on the floor of your oven. Bake for 6 to 8 minutes, until the crust is evenly brown and crisp.

Remove from the oven and top evenly with dollops of the cashew ricotta (store any extra ricotta in an airtight container in the fridge for up to 1 week). Finish with the pickled onions, slice, and serve.

GRAPEFUL DEAD

Pickled grapes on pizza? The Dead didn't follow the rules, and neither do I. Hopefully Jerry would be proud. **—PG**

Makes one 12-inch pie

. . . .

For the House-Pickled Grapes

½ cup red wine vinegar, plus more as needed

½ cup sugar

¼ teaspoon fine sea salt

½ teaspoon whole black peppercorns

1 pound seedless red grapes, cut in half

For the Pizza

1 round NY-Style Dough (page 22) or your favorite pizza dough (about ½ pound)

Semolina, for dusting

1½ cups shredded vegan mozzarella

2 cups baby spinach leaves

Olive oil (extra-virgin not necessary), for drizzling

NOTE

You'll need to think ahead when making this pie, as the grapes have to pickle for at least 8 hours. After that, you'll be ready to whip up a Grapeful Dead whenever the mood strikes, or instead of one of those baked Brie things people insist on serving at parties.

Make the house-pickled grapes: In a medium saucepan, combine the vinegar, sugar, and salt. Cook over high heat, stirring, until the sugar and salt have completely dissolved.

Place the peppercorns in a piece of cheesecloth and tie it closed with butcher's twine. (A perforated stainless-steel tea holder or really any food-grade item that will keep the peppercorns contained would also work.) Add the bundled peppercorns to the pot and bring the mixture to a boil. Remove from the heat and let the pickling liquid cool to room temperature.

Place the grapes in a heatproof large container. Pour over the cooled pickling liquid, making sure all the grapes are submerged. Top with extra vinegar if needed. Cover the container and refrigerate for at least 8 hours before using. (The grapes can be stored in their pickling liquid in the fridge for up to 1 week.)

Make the pizza: Place a pizza stone or steel on the floor of your oven. Preheat the oven to 550°F or as high as it will go for 45 minutes.

Place the dough on a pizza paddle that's been dusted with semolina and stretch it to about 12 inches. Evenly scatter the mozzarella on top. Toss the spinach with a drizzle of olive oil, then scatter the leaves on top of the pie, followed by ½ cup of the pickled grapes.

Use the paddle to transfer the pie to the pizza stone or steel on the oven floor. Bake for 6 to 8 minutes, until the crust is evenly brown and crisp and the cheese begins to brown slightly. Slice and serve.

IN RICOTTA DA VEGAN

```
Makes one 12-inch pie
```

There's a reason I named an entire chapter after this pie. It's the embodiment of what Paulie Gee's is about: a commitment to quality, killer vegan options, and clever names. —PG

∙∙

For the Vegan Sausage

½ cup extra-virgin olive oil, plus more as needed

1 large red onion, finely chopped

4 cups vital wheat gluten, preferably Bob's Red Mill

1 cup plain vegan breadcrumbs, such as Whole Foods 365

1 cup nutritional yeast

3 tablespoons fennel seeds

1 tablespoon fine sea salt

4 cups vegetable broth

For the Pizza

1 round NY-Style Dough (page 22) or your favorite pizza dough (about ½ pound)

Semolina, for dusting

½ cup Vegan Tomato Sauce (see page 91) or your favorite sauce

Cashew Ricotta (see page 99)

Handful of arugula

Extra-virgin olive oil, for drizzling

Make the vegan sausage: Bring a large pot of water to a boil over high heat. Meanwhile, drizzle some EVOO into a small saucepan and heat over medium-high heat. Add the onion and cook until golden brown and caramelized, about 5 minutes.

In a large bowl, stir together the wheat gluten, breadcrumbs, nutritional yeast, fennel seeds, and salt to combine. Add the caramelized onion, broth, and the ½ cup EVOO and knead with your hands until all the ingredients are well incorporated. Do not overwork the mixture or the end result will be too tight.

Divide the mixture in half and form each portion into a loaf. Set each loaf in the center of a piece of cheesecloth—measuring about 2 feet each—and wrap them completely, leaving about 1 inch of excess cheesecloth at the ends. Tie the excess cheesecloth closed with butcher's twine, then tie an additional two or three pieces of twine around the circumference of the loaves.

Place the loaves in the pot of boiling water, then reduce the heat to maintain a steady simmer. Partially cover the pot and simmer for 1½ hours.

Preheat the oven to 350°F.

Using tongs, carefully remove the loaves from the boiling water. Remove the twine and cheesecloth and place the loaves on a baking sheet. Bake for about 10 minutes, until golden brown (they don't need to be crispy, just brown). Remove from the oven and let cool completely before using.

Chop enough of the vegan sausage to measure 1½ cups and set aside. The remaining sausage can be wrapped tightly in plastic wrap and stored in the refrigerator for up to 5 days.

NOTE

You'll need 4 feet of cheesecloth and butcher's twine to make the vegan sausage. Once made, only chop up as much as you'll need for the pie. Keep the rest tightly wrapped in plastic in the fridge, and use within 5 days.

Make the pizza: Place a pizza stone or steel on the floor of your oven. Preheat the oven to 550°F or as high as it will go for 45 minutes.

Place the dough on a pizza paddle that's been dusted with semolina and stretch it to about 12 inches. Spread the sauce evenly over the dough, followed by the chopped vegan sausage. Use the paddle to transfer the pie to the pizza stone or steel on the oven floor. Bake for 6 to 8 minutes, until the crust is evenly brown and crisp. Top the pie with dollops of ricotta. Toss the arugula with a drizzle of olive oil, then scatter it evenly over the pie. Slice and serve.

VEGAN SHSH-SHISHIDIO

Makes one 12-inch pie

Paulie finds inspiration everywhere. In this case, it was coming from a display of shishito peppers at the supermarket. He couldn't resist picking some up to experiment with.

We make three versions of this pie. The original Shsh-Shishidio is made with regular Parm, so feel free to try it that way if you're not vegan. There's also the Wild Honey Pie, which was created for Eric Weiner's upstate New York music festival of the same name. What could be better than PG pizza and a show? It's exactly the same recipe as this one, just sweetened after the pie comes out of the oven with a swirl of vegan honey—Mellody Plant-Based Honey is our preferred brand. —MG

1 round NY-Style Dough (page 22) or your favorite pizza dough (about ½ pound)

Semolina, for dusting

1 cup shredded vegan Parmesan

20 shishito peppers, charred (see Note)

Fresh lemon juice

NOTE

Blitz the shishitos under the broiler for a few minutes, until they begin to soften and develop charred spots, then slice them into thick rounds before putting them on the pie.

Place a pizza stone or steel on the floor of your oven. Preheat the oven to 550°F or as high as it will go for 45 minutes.

Place the dough on a pizza paddle that's been dusted with semolina and stretch it to about 12 inches. Evenly scatter the Parm across the pie so there are no "dry" dough spots. Place two-thirds of the pepper slices in a big ring around the outside of the pie and the remaining peppers in a smaller ring inside the outer ring.

Use the paddle to transfer the pie to the pizza stone or steel on the oven floor. Bake for 6 to 8 minutes, until the crust is evenly brown and crisp.

Remove from the oven and squeeze some lemon juice over the pie. Slice and serve.

CHAPTER FOUR

PIES FROM OUR FAMILY OF PIZZAPRENEURS

"When you're working for someone else, you are working for someone else's dreams."

When someone opens up a Paulie Gee's franchise or one of our New York–style Slice Shops, I'm giving them a platform. Sure, we'll help with getting them open and provide them with the recipes for the tried-and-true pies that have been successful at our place. But these people don't want to be just a cookie-cutter Paulie Gee's, and we don't want them to be.

So maybe they'll start with about two-thirds of our menu before coming up with their own pies, using the same guiding principles. You'll see them do a lot of sweet and savory. Also, I'll share my list of prohibited P's that I don't think should ever be put on pizza. And one of those P's is peas! There's also poultry, pasta, and pepperoni. At Paulie Gee's, you don't put pepperoni on pizza. Prosciutto, yes, but no pepperoni.

Anyway, I have this big list of forbidden toppings. And the franchise guys have fun with it. Our guy in Chicago came up with a pie called Paulie's Prohibited. Every month there'll be a pie with a different prohibited ingredient from my list. And these franchises pay homage to me with cute names for their pizzas. The Hot Child in the City and the Dollop Parton in Baltimore. The Joe Peppitoni and the Big Cheesy in Columbus. And the Say Chowdah and the Netflix and Chilee in Chicago. These are pies they came up with themselves. They've taken my lead by expressing themselves through their pizza the way I express myself through mine. **—PG**

Paulie's Playlist

"Soul City Walk," Archie Bell and the Drells

"The Love I Lost," Harold Melvin and the Blue Notes

"I'll Always Love My Mama," The Intruders

"Listen," Chicago

"We're a Winner," Curtis Mayfield and the Impressions

"One Night Affair," Jerry Butler

"Can't Get Enough of Your Love, Babe," Barry White

"Way Down in the Hole," The Blind Boys of Alabama

"My Babe," Columbus Short

"Fire," Ohio Players

"New York State of Mind," Billy Joel

"I Guess the Lord Must Be in New York City," Harry Nilsson

"Brooklyn," Youngblood Brass Band

THE FAMILY OF FRANCHISES

PAULIE GEE'S SLICE SHOP, BROOKLYN, NY

NY slice shops were such a big part of our childhood and young adult life. So while Neapolitan-style pizzas were the first thing Paulie experimented with professionally, he knew he eventually wanted to be able to pay homage to the classic pizza parlors we grew up with in Brooklyn. Our Slice Shops have really resonated with our guests, too—so many of them comment on how they remind them of their youth, not just in Brooklyn, but all over the country. **—MG**

PAULIE GEE'S SLICE SHOP, PHILADELPHIA, PA

Jake Resnik, Founding Pizza Maker, Philly: I started out at Paulie's original Greenpoint restaurant in 2017, fresh out of my first year of college. Interview day, I discussed culinary school with Paulie and his reply was "Don't need that. You'll learn everything you need to know here." Is now an okay time to tell you guys one of my references was fake?

I quickly transitioned from prep work to full-time pizzaiolo, and by the time Paulie's first Slice Shop in Brooklyn was finally ready to open, I wanted nothing more than to be a part of it. I grew up on Long Island, and that style of pizza was an integral part of my childhood. I became one of the main guys over there right when COVID hit, and I was proud to be able to help people find a sense of normalcy during a difficult time.

PAULIE GEE'S CHICAGO (LOGAN SQUARE, WICKER PARK, WHEELING, AND PAULIE GEE'S CATERING)

MG: We opened up our Logan Square full-service restaurant in 2016, as an expansion of what we created at 60 Greenpoint. The Wicker Park Slice Shop followed in 2021—a fast-casual spot in one of the most interesting intersections in the city— and our catering program came soon after that on the heels of the pandemic, when we realized we needed to grow a separate arm of the business. The amazing Derrick Tung runs all four.

Derrick Tung, Owner of Paulie Gee's Logan Square, Wicker Park, Wheeling, and Catering: My relationship with Paulie started like any good relationship in the millennium. I swiped right. Okay, not exactly, but we did meet online.

I'd just finished my first summer season selling wood-fired Neapolitan-inspired pizzas at local farmers' markets and private events, and I was looking for a mentor to guide me toward eventually opening a restaurant. Paulie had just done an interview with *Eater*, and had basically put out his contact information saying that if anyone wanted to talk mentorship, he'd be happy to chat. So I reached out, and over time, we decided that we wanted to work together to open up a franchise in Chicago.

Paulie has been great about giving us a wide berth to adjust our own business models, develop our own leadership styles, and approach pizza in a way that reflects our own personalities. And Mary Ann has always been a strong source of encouragement, cheering us on as we continue to grow, and making sure we carve out enough time for our families outside of the restaurant. It's been an amazing learning experience and I value our friendship, even if we do butt heads from time to time.

PAULIE GEE'S HAMPDEN

Kelly Beckham opened Paulie Gee's Hampden in Baltimore in June 2016. He's been obsessed with pizza for practically as long as Paulie . . . he used to religiously follow Paulie's comments on the popular pizza blog *Slice New York* dating all the way back to 2003.

When he heard we were holding pizza tastings at our home in New Jersey, he joked to Paulie that he planned to get in his car and show up at our doorstep. Paulie called his bluff with an official invite, and the rest is history. **—MG**

PAULIE GEE'S SHORT NORTH

Paulie Gee's Short North was our first franchise outside the NYC area. It was opened in 2016 by TJ Gibbs, who sought out an apprenticeship with Paulie after graduating with a hospitality degree from Ohio State. He did double duty with us, learning the ins and outs of both how to make pizza as well as how to operate the front of house, before heading home to Ohio to put those skills to work.

Located in the heart of Columbus, close to the Ohio State campus, Paulie Gee's Short North was voted "Ohio's Best Pizza" by the international publication *Lovefood*, in honor of both their wood-fired and Detroit-style pies. **—MG**

NY-STYLE PIZZA

Makes one 20-inch pie

At the Slice Shop, we use hand-milled California tomatoes, no spices, and shredded part-skim low-moisture mozzarella for our classic NY slices. Nothing else. —PG

• •

1 round NY-Style Dough (page 22) or your favorite pizza dough (about 1 pound)

Semolina, for dusting

1 cup hand-milled tomatoes (see Note) or your favorite sauce (such as Vegan Tomato Sauce, page 91)

1 cup shredded part-skim low-moisture mozzarella cheese (or your favorite cheese)

Toppings of choice (if you must)

NOTE

Instead of hand-milled fresh tomatoes, you can use canned peeled tomatoes pureed in a food processor or blender, or passed through a food mill.

Remove the dough from the refrigerator 3 hours before you intend to bake it and let it sit at room temperature. About 45 minutes before baking the pie, place a pizza stone or steel on the floor of your oven. Preheat the oven to 550°F or as high as it will go.

Place the dough on a pizza paddle that's been dusted with semolina and stretch it into a 20-inch round. Top evenly with the sauce and cheese and your desired toppings (if using).

Use the paddle to transfer the pie to the pizza stone or steel on the oven floor. Bake for 6 to 8 minutes, until the dough is evenly brown and crispy and the cheese has melted.

Remove from the oven and let cool slightly before slicing and serving.

THE FREDDY PRINZE

Makes one 11 × 17-inch
rectangular pie

Andrew Brown worked at 60 Greenpoint for five years as our kitchen manager, and he wanted to open a location with us in the neighborhood. He ended up taking the lead at our very first Slice Shop, which opened in 2018. It took almost three years to build out the space.

The Freddy Prinze is one of the first pizza recipes he created, under Paulie's guidance. It takes inspiration from Freddy's in Whitestone, New York, and their sesame-crusted pies, as well as Prince Street Pizza in NYC, a shop Paulie used to visit on his commute home to New Jersey. It has been a fan favorite since we opened our doors. **—MG**

· ·

Olive oil (extra-virgin not necessary), for greasing

½ cup sesame seeds

1 round Sicilian-Style Dough (page 22) or your favorite pizza dough (about 1 pound)

1½ cups shredded part-skim low-moisture mozzarella cheese

2 ounces fresh whole-milk mozzarella cheese, sliced

1¼ cups canned crushed tomatoes or your favorite tomato sauce (such as Vegan Tomato Sauce, page 91)

Grated Pecorino Romano cheese, for sprinkling

Lightly oil an 11 × 17-inch baking pan and cover the bottom with the sesame seeds. Gently lay the dough on top of the sesame seeds, being careful not to handle the dough too much. Let the dough rise for 3 hours at room temperature, slowly stretching it to the corners of the pan every 30 minutes.

About 45 minutes before the dough has finished rising, preheat the oven to 550°F or as high as it will go.

Lightly dimple the dough with your fingers and top with the low-moisture mozzarella and the fresh mozzarella. Bake for 10 minutes, then spread the tomatoes over the cheese and bake for 15 minutes more, until the crust is golden brown throughout and crisp on the bottom.

Remove from the oven and sprinkle with pecorino. Let cool slightly before slicing and serving.

GRANDMA PIE

The recipe Paulie uses for the Grandma Pie at the Slice Shop in Brooklyn was inspired by the Grandma pie at Nino's in Bay Ridge, Brooklyn. A Grandma pie is a thin-crusted pan-baked pie typically topped with rustic crushed canned Italian-style tomatoes, cheese, and sometimes fresh garlic and oregano. He wanted to emulate that using basil oil and no garlic. —MG

Makes one 12 × 18-inch
rectangular pie

▪ ▪

Olive oil (extra-virgin not necessary), for greasing

1 round NY-Style Dough (page 22) or your favorite pizza dough (about 1 pound)

1½ cups shredded part-skim low-moisture mozzarella cheese

1¼ cups canned crushed tomatoes or your favorite sauce (such as Vegan Tomato Sauce, page 91)

1 tablespoon dried oregano

Basil oil, for drizzling (see Note)

Grated Parmigiano Reggiano or Pecorino Romano cheese, for sprinkling

Preheat the oven to 550°F or as high as it will go for 45 minutes.

Lightly oil a half sheet pan (approximately 12 × 18 × 1-inch) or baking sheet. Stretch the dough to fit the pan and set aside to proof for 30 minutes, or until the dough reaches the sides of the pan and doesn't pull back.

Lightly dimple the dough with your fingers and top with the mozzarella. Create stripes of the sauce across the surface of the cheese. Bake for about 12 minutes, until the crust is evenly brown and crispy.

Remove from the oven and sprinkle with the oregano. Drizzle with basil oil, sprinkle with Parm or pecorino, and let cool slightly before slicing and serving.

NOTE

Basil oil consists of 4 parts fresh basil to 1 part extra-virgin olive oil. One batch for us is 4 cups basil and 1 cup oil, but you can make more or less as desired. Just process the basil in a food processor and stream in the oil slowly until combined. Or you could just drizzle some torn fresh basil leaves with EVOO and scatter them over the pie.

VEGAN VIDALIA

This is an homage to the true Sicilian slice, otherwise known as sfincione. Except at the Slice Shop, we stay away from anchovies to make it vegan. —**PG**

Makes one 11 × 17-inch rectangular pie

....

1 tablespoon olive oil (extra-virgin not necessary), plus more for greasing

½ cup sesame seeds

1 round Sicilian-Style Dough (page 22) or your favorite pizza dough (about 1 pound)

1 large Vidalia onion, diced (about 2 cups)

1½ cups canned crushed tomatoes or your favorite sauce (such as Vegan Tomato Sauce, page 91)

Shredded vegan Parmesan, for sprinkling

Lightly oil an 11×17-inch baking pan and cover the bottom with the sesame seeds. Gently lay the dough over the sesame seeds, being careful not to handle the dough too much. Let the dough rise for 3 hours at room temperature, slowly stretching it to the corners of the pan every 30 minutes.

About 45 minutes before baking the pie, preheat the oven to 550°F or as high as it will go.

In a medium skillet, combine the onion and the olive oil and cook over low heat until the onion is golden brown, about 15 minutes. Remove from the heat.

Lightly dimple the dough with your fingers and top with the tomatoes, followed by the onion. Sprinkle with Parmesan.

Bake for 25 minutes, until the crust is evenly golden brown and crispy. Let cool slightly before slicing and serving.

JAKE SPECIAL NY-STYLE PIZZA

Makes one 20-inch pie

We asked one of our favorite pizza makers, Jake Resnik, to move from Brooklyn to Philly to help run the Slice Shop with our son, Derek. Jake was looking for a challenge, and boy, did he live up to it, even coming up with one of the most defining pies on the menu. —MG

· ·

1 round NY-Style Dough (page 22) or your favorite pizza dough (about 1 pound)

Semolina, for dusting

1 cup canned crushed tomatoes, preferably Tomato Magic Ground Tomatoes

1 cup shredded part-skim low-moisture mozzarella cheese

1 cup sliced hot cherry peppers

6½ ounces or about 2½ links sweet Italian sausage, sliced (I like Fontanini brand)

¼ medium red onion, thinly sliced (about ¼ cup)

2 tablespoons grated Pecorino Romano cheese

Freshly cracked black pepper

Place a pizza stone or steel on the floor of your oven. Preheat the oven to 550°F or as high as it will go for 45 minutes.

Stretch the dough into a 20-inch round on top of a pizza paddle that's been dusted with semolina (or on a lightly greased pan). Top with the tomatoes, followed by the mozzarella, cherry peppers, sausage, and onion.

Launch your pie directly onto the pizza stone or steel and bake for 8 to 12 minutes, depending on how hot your oven is, until the crust is golden brown and crispy on the bottom and the cheese has melted.

Remove from the oven, slice, and finish with the pecorino and a generous amount of black pepper.

BACON ALFREDO NY-STYLE PIZZA

Makes one 20-inch pie

Paul Brancale created this recipe. He's another beloved alum of 60 Greenpoint and our Brooklyn Slice Shop who went on to help open our Slice Shop in Philly. You'll definitely want to use any leftover Alfredo sauce to make more pizzas, or pair it with your favorite pasta. —MG

For the Alfredo Sauce

½ cup (1 stick) salted butter

1 garlic head, cloves separated, peeled, and minced

2 cups heavy cream

1 cup grated Pecorino Romano cheese

Freshly ground black pepper

For the Pizza

8 ounces wood-smoked bacon strips

1 round NY-Style Dough (page 22) or your favorite pizza dough (about 1 pound)

Semolina, for dusting

1 cup shredded part-skim low-moisture mozzarella cheese

Freshly ground black pepper

Make the Alfredo sauce: Melt the butter in a medium saucepan over medium heat. Add the garlic and cook, stirring occasionally, until soft and fragrant, about 4 minutes, being careful not to let it burn. Transfer the contents of the pan to a blender and add the cream, pecorino, and about 10 twists of pepper. Blend for about 30 seconds to combine.

Make the pizza: Place a pizza stone or steel on the floor of your oven. Preheat the oven to 550°F or as high as it will go for 45 minutes.

Cook the bacon using your desired method, just until the fat has rendered but before the bacon gets crispy. Coarsely chop.

Stretch the dough into a 14-inch round on top of a pizza paddle that's been dusted with semolina (or on a lightly greased pan). Top with about ½ cup of the Alfredo and evenly sprinkle the mozzarella on top of that. Fully cover the top with the bacon.

Launch your pie directly onto the pizza stone or steel and bake for 8 to 15 minutes, until the cheese has melted, the bacon is crisp, and the crust is evenly brown and crisp throughout.

Remove from the oven and finish with pepper. Slice and serve.

NETFLIX AND CHILEE

Makes one 12-inch pie

Derrik Tung is the owner of Paulie Gee's Logan Square, Wicker Park, and Wheeling in Chicago. And he's a great example of how our franchise partners have really put themselves on the menu while remaining true to the spirit of Paulie Gee's. Inspired by the pork floss sandwiches his maternal grandmother used to love, it became Derrik's mission to find a way to top pizza with the dried shredded meat. Also known as hairy pork, rou song, or pork sung, pork floss has a cotton candy texture and a sweet and sugary flavor, and can be commonly found in Asian markets.

While Derrik's mom called his first attempt one of the worst pizzas he'd ever made, he eventually combined pork floss with house-pickled pineapple, some locally made chili crisp, and sliced raw red onion for a pizza that's not only beautiful to look at, but perfectly highlights pork floss. And it's ideal to have while watching Netflix and "chileeing" at home! —MG

---

1 round NY-Style Dough (page 22) or your favorite pizza dough (about ½ pound)

Semolina, for dusting

4 ounces shredded low-moisture mozzarella cheese

1 garlic head, cloves separated, peeled, and sliced

⅓ cup Pickled Pineapple (see page 49), drained

Chili crisp (we prefer Chilee Crisp brand, made in Chicago)

Small handful of pork floss

¼ medium red onion, thinly sliced

Place a pizza stone or steel on the floor of your oven. Preheat the oven to 550°F or as high as it will go for 45 minutes.

Place the dough on a pizza paddle that's been dusted with semolina and stretch it to about 12 inches. Top with the mozzarella, followed by the garlic and the pickled pineapple.

Use the paddle to transfer the pie to the pizza stone or steel on the oven floor. Bake for 6 to 8 minutes, until the cheese is melted and the crust is evenly brown and crispy throughout.

Remove from the oven and let cool slightly. Add spoonfuls of chili crisp to taste, making sure to evenly distribute them across the pie. Add the pork floss to the pie, sprinkling it from above to aid in even distribution. Lay the onion slices across the pie, slice, and serve.

THRILLA IN MANILA

Makes one 12-inch pie

One of Derrik's goals has been to introduce more Asian flavors to the gourmet pizza world, something that was definitely lacking when we opened in 2016. This particular pie is inspired by his favorite Filipino breakfast, longsilog. It features garlic fried rice, Filipino longanisa sausage, over-easy eggs, and sawsawan (essentially Filipino salsa). The fattiness and richness of the sausage and eggs are cut with the sawsawan and rounded out by flavorful garlic rice (or in this case, pizza crust), which makes for an amazing balance in flavors. —MG

For the Sawsawan

¼ cup soy sauce

2 tablespoons sugarcane vinegar, preferably Datu Puti brand

½ teaspoon calamansi juice, or 1 tablespoon fresh lemon juice

2 fresh bird's-eye chiles or other spicy peppers

1 medium Roma tomato, seeded and diced

1 medium red onion, diced (about 2 cups)

For the Pizza

3 large egg yolks

3 links Filipino longanisa

1 round NY-Style Dough (page 22) or your favorite pizza dough (about ½ pound)

Semolina, for dusting

1 cup hand-milled tomatoes (see Note, page 113) or your favorite tomato sauce (such as Vegan Tomato Sauce, page 91)

1 cup shredded low-moisture mozzarella cheese

2 garlic heads, cloves separated, peeled, and sliced

Make the sawsawan: In a medium bowl, stir together the soy sauce, vinegar, calamansi juice, chiles, tomato, onion, and 2 tablespoons water. Refrigerate until ready to use.

Make the pizza: Using an immersion circulator, heat a water bath to 150°F. Place the egg yolks in a vacuum-seal bag, seal, and cook in the water bath for 1 hour, until thickened but still runny (see Note).

Place a pizza stone or steel on the floor of your oven. Preheat the oven to 550°F or as high as it will go for 45 minutes.

Cook the longanisa, either by removing the casings and pan-frying the meat in crumbles, or pan-frying the links whole, then slicing them into medallions. Place the dough on a pizza paddle that's been dusted with semolina and stretch it to about 12 inches. Top with the tomatoes, then the mozzarella, garlic, and longanisa.

Use the paddle to transfer the pie to the pizza stone or steel on the oven floor. Bake for 6 to 8 minutes, until the crust is evenly brown and crisp and the cheese begins to brown. Remove from the oven and let cool slightly before slicing. Cut the tip off of the egg yolk bag. Drizzle egg yolk across the topped part of the pizza, taking care to avoid the crust. Using a slotted spoon, scoop the sawsawan over the pizza and serve right away.

NOTE

Instead of cooking the egg yolks sous vide, you can prepare 3 whole eggs soft-boiled or sunny-side-up and place them on top of the pie.

BARRY WHITE

Makes one 12-inch pie

One of Kelly Beckham's (of Paulie Gee's Hampden) favorite things is cacio e pepe, a Roman pasta dish featuring black pepper, cheese, and little else. It inspired him to create this pie, which he first tried out on his own backyard grill and eventually added a drizzle of Paulie's Aleppo chile oil to the mix for an earthy, spicy kick that pairs well with the elegantly simple combo of pepper and cheese. —MG

For the Garlic Oil

¼ cup extra-virgin olive oil

4 garlic cloves, peeled

For the Pizza

1 round NY-Style Dough (page 22) or your favorite pizza dough (about ½ pound)

Semolina, for dusting

1 cup shredded whole-milk low-moisture mozzarella cheese

1½ ounces fresh whole-milk mozzarella cheese, sliced

¼ cup grated Pecorino Romano cheese

¼ cup grated Parmigiano Reggiano cheese

Aleppo Chile Oil (see page 91), for drizzling

Freshly ground black pepper

Make the garlic oil: In a small skillet, heat the olive oil and garlic over low heat. Cook, stirring occasionally and making sure the heat stays low enough that the oil doesn't simmer, for 30 minutes. Raise the heat to bring the oil to a simmer and cook until the garlic just starts to brown. Remove the pan from the heat. Remove the garlic cloves and let the oil cool before using.

Make the pizza: Place a pizza stone or steel on the floor of your oven. Preheat the oven to 550°F or as high as it will go for 45 minutes.

Place the dough on a pizza paddle that's been dusted with semolina and stretch it to about 12 inches. Top with the shredded mozzarella and the sliced fresh mozzarella, followed by the pecorino and Parm. Drizzle with the garlic oil.

Use the paddle to transfer the pie to the pizza stone or steel on the oven floor. Bake for 6 to 8 minutes, until the cheese is melted and the crust is evenly brown and crispy throughout.

Remove from the oven and finish with a drizzle of Aleppo chile oil and a sprinkle of pepper. Let cool slightly before slicing and serving.

SHERRY LEE LEWIS SALAD

This cool-weather salad was developed specifically for our Hampden location, and it makes the most of the high-quality ingredients our restaurants are known for. Which means, make the effort to find the best guanciale you can. We prefer Salumeria Biellese brand. —MG

Serves 4

For the Oloroso Sherry Vinaigrette

¾ cup medium dry oloroso sherry (we prefer Barbadillo brand)

½ cup wildflower or clover honey

½ cup white wine vinegar

¼ cup plus 2 tablespoons Dijon mustard

Fine sea salt and coarsely ground black pepper

For the Salad

4 thinly sliced strips guanciale (about 4 ounces)

4 cups loosely packed spring mix (16 ounces)

¼ medium red onion, very thinly sliced

¼ cup dried cranberries

¼ cup Candied Pecans (see page 151)

Fine sea salt and coarsely ground black pepper

Make the vinaigrette: In a medium bowl or a blender, combine the sherry, honey, vinegar, mustard, and salt and pepper to taste. Whisk or blend until fully incorporated. Set aside.

Make the salad: Place the guanciale in a small pan. Cook over medium heat until brown and bubbling, about 5 minutes. Use tongs or a slotted spoon to transfer the guanciale to a paper towel–lined plate, reserving the rendered fat in the pan.

In a large bowl, combine the spring mix, onion, and most of the cranberries and pecans (reserve a small amount of each for garnish). Add the guanciale and the rendered fat from the pan, along with ¼ cup of the vinaigrette. Use tongs to mix until everything is well combined. Divide among four plates, topping each serving with a sprinkle of salt, a couple twists of pepper, and a few of the reserved cranberries and pecans.

VEGAN BEET BALLS

Makes about 1 dozen balls

These beet balls from our Hamden location are meant to be enjoyed as a topping for pizza (i.e., not as a vegan alternative for meatballs). That's because they're best when cooked directly on the pizza in the oven. If you try to sauté them or cook them another way to serve on spaghetti, they come out very dry. —PG

For the Spice Blend

¼ cup dried oregano

¼ cup Aleppo chile flakes

¼ cup red pepper flakes

¼ cup kosher salt

¼ cup fennel seeds

2 tablespoons sweet paprika

2 tablespoons ground cumin

2 tablespoons coarsely ground black pepper

⅛ teaspoon cayenne pepper

For the Beet Balls

2 tablespoons olive oil (extra-virgin not necessary)

1 medium red onion, diced

3 garlic cloves, peeled

2 cups almonds, toasted

2 medium beets, peeled, steamed, and chopped (about 1 cup)

1 cup breadcrumbs

1 cup nutritional yeast

Make the spice blend: In a bowl, combine all the spice blend ingredients with a fork. Set aside.

Make the beet balls: In a medium sauté pan, combine the olive oil and the onion and cook over medium-high heat, stirring occasionally, until the onion is golden and fragrant, 8 to 10 minutes. Add the garlic cloves and cook until they're golden, about 4 minutes more.

In a food processor, grind the almonds until they have the texture of breadcrumbs, then transfer them to a large bowl. In the food processor, combine the onion and garlic with the beets and process into a paste. Add the beet mixture to the bowl with the almonds, then add the breadcrumbs, nutritional yeast, and ¼ cup of the spice blend (see Note). Fold everything together by hand until combined; it should have a texture similar to Play-Doh once cooled. The beet mixture can be stored in an airtight container in the fridge for up to 1 week.

When ready to use, give small handfuls of the beet mixture a loose roll in your hands so they form balls. Tear little clumps from the balls and place them on top of your pizza. Bake the pizza as directed.

NOTE

Leftover spice blend can be stored in an airtight container in a cool, dry place for up to a year.

BRISKET MARMALADE

Use this as a topping for pizza or crostini. It's especially delicious paired with whipped feta cheese and Pickled Red Onions (see page 46). —MG

Makes 3 cups

· ·

½ cup plus 2 tablespoons ketchup

½ cup plus 2 tablespoons red wine

¼ cup plus 1 tablespoon red wine vinegar

¼ cup plus 1 tablespoon apple cider vinegar

1½ tablespoons tomato paste

1 tablespoon rye whiskey

1 tablespoon brown sugar

1 tablespoon honey

2 teaspoons minced garlic

1 sprig rosemary

1½ pounds of your favorite locally smoked brisket, fat trimmed, cut into small cubes

In a large pot, combine the ketchup, wine, red wine vinegar, apple cider vinegar, tomato paste, whiskey, brown sugar, honey, garlic, and rosemary. Bring to a simmer over medium heat and cook until slightly thickened, 30 to 45 minutes. Stir in the brisket and simmer for 30 minutes more to allow the flavors to meld. Remove from the heat and let cool to room temperature before using or storing. Store in an airtight container in the fridge for up to 5 days.

CHAPTER FIVE

SECOND ACTS

"The only thing constant in life is change."

The name of the game here is contrast. When it comes to what I serve at the restaurant, well, everything has been designed to contrast the pizza. So you won't find any other form of bread anywhere on the menu. No bruschetta. No breadsticks. Instead, you can order butter—cold, salted butter only—to put directly on your crust.

I apply the same philosophy to what I make at home. Whether it's a hot soup, a cold salad, or a vegetable, it should complement the main course. Fill in the blanks based on what your menu lacks.

And by the way, I don't make anything I don't love just because people ask for it. Life is too short for that. That's why you'll find recipes for all my favorites here. Savory soups with a surprising hint of sweetness. Chopped salads that are as unique as my playlists. And I don't just allow any old song to make it onto my playlist. **—PG**

Paulie's Playlist

"Spain (I Can Recall)," Al Jarreau

"C'mon Marianne," The Four Seasons

"Gates of Eden," Bob Dylan

"Going to Mexico," Steve Miller Band

"Autumn in New York," Frank Sinatra

"French Roast," Lee Ritenour

"Last Tango in Paris," Neil Larsen

"Parisienne Walkways," Gary Moore

GATES OF EDEN

I used to make a version of this salad for our home pizza tastings. Our guests would always comment on how I made the best salads. Paulie gets to lay claim to pizza, but cold foods are really my speciality. —MG

Serves 2

∎∎

For the Vinaigrette

1¼ cups Minute Maid Berry Punch (yes, really)

¼ cup extra-virgin olive oil

¼ cup red wine vinegar

For the Salad

2 cups mixed greens

½ cup crumbled Gorgonzola cheese

½ Bosc pear, thinly sliced

¼ cup thinly sliced red onion

¼ cup dried cherries or cranberries (see Note)

¼ cup Candied Pecans (see page 151)

Make the vinaigrette: In a medium bowl, whisk together the punch, olive oil, and vinegar until fully blended.

Make the salad: In a large bowl, combine the greens, cheese, pear, onion, cherries, and pecans. Pour the vinaigrette over the top and toss to coat. Divide between two salad plates, making sure that some of the goodies (onion, nuts, fruit, cheese) are plated on top of the greens.

NOTE

Dried cranberries make the salad taste just as good and are a lot cheaper than dried cherries.

BELMONT

Serves 4

We used to close on Mondays during the early days of the restaurant. So whenever Paulie decided not to trek into Brooklyn (which he often did anyway), we reserved that time to dine out with friends. And Belmont Tavern in Belleville, New Jersey, was (and still is) a favorite.

The old-school Italian joint is in the town where Frankie Valli and the Four Seasons grew up. It's still run by the family of the original owner, and has the red checkered tablecloths, a classic jukebox spinning tunes, and the best Italian food.

While they're famous for their Stretch's Chicken Savoy (sprinkled with cheese, roasted, and finished with vinegar sauce), it's this salad that we loved so much that we just had to pay homage to it on our menu. Ours has Pecorino Romano cheese in it (because it's what Paulie always requests be added to his salad at the Belmont), and people ask us all the time for the salad dressing recipe. It's delicious! —MG

1 head escarole, well cleaned and cut into bite-size pieces (see Note)

1 cup shredded Pecorino Romano cheese

1 cup extra-virgin olive oil

6 tablespoons red wine vinegar

6 garlic cloves, peeled

Place the escarole in a large serving bowl.

In a food processor, combine the cheese, olive oil, vinegar, garlic, and 6 tablespoons water. Process until smooth, then pour the dressing over the escarole. Toss until evenly coated and serve.

NOTE

Escarole tends to be sandy, so you'll need to clean it thoroughly and run it through a salad spinner a few times to make sure all the grit is gone.

CHEEK COREA

Serves 2

I named a guanciale pizza after one of my favorite basketball players, Mo Cheeks (see page 56), and as extra credit, he got a salad, too. Okay, he has to share the honor with the great jazz musician Chick Corea. You know how I feel about musical names. —PG

. . . .

½ cup cubed guanciale

2 cups escarole, washed well (see Note, page 142)

2 cups chilled cooked ditalini pasta

½ small red onion, thinly sliced

½ cup cooked chickpeas (see Note)

Fresh lemon juice, for drizzling

Extra-virgin olive oil, for drizzling

Aleppo Chile Oil (see page 91), for drizzling

In a small pan, cook the guanciale over high heat until it is crisped and brown and the fat has rendered out, about 5 minutes. Transfer the guanciale to a paper towel–lined plate to drain, reserving the rendered fat in the pan.

In a large bowl, combine the escarole, pasta, onion, and chickpeas. Drizzle with lemon juice, olive oil, and chile oil and mix well to combine.

Divide the salad between two plates and scatter the crisped guanciale on top. Drizzle a bit of the reserved guanciale fat over each salad and serve.

NOTE

We cook our own chickpeas, but we won't look at you sideways if you don't feel like doing the same. Canned is fine. If you do feel like going for it, soak dried chickpeas for at least 12 hours, then drain them and put them in a big pot. Add cold water to cover, a few cloves of garlic, a few strips of lemon peel, and a couple of bay leaves. Bring to a boil over high heat, reduce the heat to maintain a simmer, cover, and cook for 1½ hours. Season with salt during the last 30 minutes of cooking (if you salt too early, it will slow down the cooking process). Drain and use as you like, or store in an airtight container in the fridge for 3 to 5 days.

CHILLED WATERMELON SOUP

Paulie created this soup for our summertime menus. He played around with the recipe for a while, because he wanted something sweet yet refreshing that wasn't another pizza or salad. This is also a winner because it's easy to execute in terms of time and labor. —MG

Serves 2 to 4

∙∙

4 cups chopped seedless watermelon, plus more for garnish

2 tablespoons fresh lemon juice

1 tablespoon chopped fresh mint, plus whole leaves for garnish

1½ teaspoons agave nectar

¼ teaspoon fine sea salt

Combine the watermelon, lemon juice, mint, agave, and salt in a blender and blend on high until smooth. Divide the soup among bowls and garnish each serving with a few pieces of watermelon and some mint leaves.

GAZPACHO

Serves 6 to 8

This is a refreshing soup we love to make at home and serve on a hot summer day. It's a delicious accompaniment to barbecue. The other plus is it allows us to make use of ingredients we always have on hand, namely Tomato Magic. As I mentioned before, if you can't get ahold of Tomato Magic, see page 16. —MG

6 cups canned crushed Italian tomatoes, preferably Tomato Magic Ground Tomatoes

¼ cup extra-virgin olive oil, plus more for serving

1 medium red onion, chopped

12 garlic cloves, peeled

2 cucumbers, peeled, seeded, and finely chopped (reserve some for garnish)

¼ cup red wine vinegar

1 teaspoon fine sea salt

1 teaspoon Aleppo Chile Oil (see page 91)

In a food processor, combine 3 cups of the tomatoes, the olive oil, onion, garlic, cucumbers, vinegar, salt, and Aleppo chile oil. Blend until smooth.

Pour into a large bowl, add the remaining 3 cups tomatoes and 4 cups water, and whisk vigorously to combine. Chill the gazpacho in the fridge for at least 2 hours before serving.

Serve individual portions in bowls, drizzled with olive oil and garnished with a few pieces of chopped cucumber.

PUMPKIN BISQUE

Serves 10 to 12

We love lobster bisque, but who can afford to make it all the time? That's why I came up with this pumpkin bisque recipe, so we could enjoy this style of soup more regularly at home. We also love pecans, and you can basically use the candied pecans we make for a garnish on anything: soups, salads, ice cream—go wild. —PG

▪▪

For the Candied Pecans

¾ cup packed dark or light brown sugar

2 cups salted pecans

For the Bisque

½ cup (1 stick) salted butter

1 large Vidalia onion, diced

2 cups sherry cooking wine

5 cups vegetable broth (not low-sodium)

2 cups heavy cream

24 ounces canned pumpkin puree

¾ cup packed dark or light brown sugar

Pumpkin pie spice

NOTE

We use 29-ounce cans of Libby's pure pumpkin puree, which means there's about 5 ounces of puree left over. We like to freeze it for later use, like making muffins.

Make the candied pecans: In a large skillet, combine the brown sugar and ¼ cup water. Cook over high heat until a syrup forms, about 2 minutes. Add the nuts and stir to coat. Reduce the heat to medium and cook, stirring frequently, until the syrup has turned thick and sticky, about 5 minutes. DO NOT LET IT BURN. Use a spatula to transfer the pecans to a wire rack and let cool at room temperature. The pecans can be stored in an airtight container at room temperature for up to 2 weeks.

Make the bisque: In a medium pot, melt the butter over low heat. Add the onion and cook until browned and translucent, about 12 minutes. Pour in the sherry and increase the heat to medium. Cook for 5 minutes, being sure to scrape up any caramelized bits of onion from the bottom of the pan.

Add the broth, cream, pumpkin puree, brown sugar, and a few shakes of pumpkin pie spice to the pot, stirring to make sure all the ingredients, especially the brown sugar, are fully incorporated. Increase the heat to high and bring the bisque to a boil, then turn the burner off and let the bisque cool for a few minutes.

Carefully transfer the bisque to a blender or food processor and blend on high until smooth, 45 to 75 seconds. (Alternatively, blend the bisque directly in the pot using an immersion blender.)

Serve hot, garnishing each serving with some of the candied pecans.

VEGETARIAN FRENCH ONION SOUP

Serves 8 to 10

French onion soup generally includes beef broth, which is how we make it at home. But we're always looking to provide vegetarian options for our guests at the restaurant, which is why I started using vegetable broth. And I still contend that this version is the best French onion soup I've ever had. Just make sure you have enough sliced bread and shredded cheese on hand for everyone you're serving. —PG

· ·

1 cup (2 sticks) salted butter

⅓ cup olive oil (extra-virgin not necessary)

11 Vidalia onions, thinly sliced

6 cups vegetable broth

8 to 10 slices French baguette

Shredded Swiss cheese

NOTE

Depending on how many people you plan to serve, you'll probably have leftovers—which is a great thing, because this soup freezes well for up to 6 months, or can be kept in the fridge in an airtight container for up to 5 days.

In a large pot, melt the butter over medium heat. Add the olive oil and onions, reduce the heat to medium-low, and cook until the onions are deeply caramelized, about 30 minutes.

Add the broth, increase the heat to high, and bring to a boil. Reduce the heat to medium and simmer for 5 minutes.

Preheat the broiler.

Place a slice of bread in the bottom of each individual ovenproof crock or bowl. Ladle in enough broth from the pot to cover the bread, then spoon in enough onions to fill each crock to the rim. Sprinkle a handful of cheese over the top of each serving. Place the crocks on a baking sheet and slide them under the broiler. Broil just until the cheese browns, then remove from the oven and serve.

ARNOLD BROTHSTEIN 2.0

Serves 1

This is a vegan version of our original Arnold Brothstein soup, which I served when we first opened as a way to use up left-over Parmigiano cheese rinds. They happened to be filming the show *Boardwalk Empire* in the neighborhood around that time, so I named it after my favorite character.

Not only is this soup delicious, it's also so simple to make, and it's a great way to use leftovers from the other recipes we've included in the book. The ratios are for one person, since it comes together in the microwave, but you can double, triple, quadruple it . . . you know the drill. —PG

½ cup coarsely chopped escarole (see Note, page 142)

¾ cup cooked ditalini pasta

¼ cup Vegan Tomato Sauce (see page 91)

¼ cup Vegan Sausage (see page 102)

Drizzle of Aleppo Chile Oil (see page 91)

1 cup vegetable broth (not low-sodium)

Place all the ingredients in a small microwave-safe soup bowl. Microwave on high for 2 minutes 15 seconds, until warmed through. Serve immediately.

THE OVEN THAT STARTED IT ALL

When we talk about second acts, well, mine began by building my very own wood-fired pizza oven in my very own New Jersey backyard. At first, I considered having someone else build it for me. But that's a costly proposition. So I did a little research and, believe it or not, you can find free Pompeii oven plans on FornoBravo.com. (Significant others . . . if you suddenly find yourself with a wood-burning oven in your backyard, don't look at me.)

I started with an existing stone base that the previous homeowner had been using as a BBQ staging area, and then I purchased a bunch of fire bricks. I had to rent a brick cutter to split them in half, and when Mary Ann came home and saw the bricks and the cutter, she asked what I was doing. Okay, maybe not as casually or as nicely as that. I told her I was building a pizza oven and her reply was, "What am I going to do with my plants?"

My sons were much more excited. In fact, while I thought I was making decent progress despite having limited time to work on it (and not being a professional wood-burning oven builder), my son Michael wasn't impressed. Toward the end of October, he told me that he was bringing his roommate home for Thanksgiving and, in no uncertain terms, stated that he wanted pizza out of the oven. He threw the gauntlet down at me, saying, "You can't talk shit and not do something about it."

That challenge was a gift. The oven may not have been visually stunning by the time Michael and his roommate arrived, but you better believe it was in working condition just in time for Thanksgiving. —**PG**

CHAPTER SIX

THE WALL OF FAME

"Nothing is invented, only discovered."

PG: It all started when I asked Chris Bianco if I should buy or make my own mozzarella. And he told me, in no uncertain terms, that if you support other people, they'll support you.

MG: That's why we've always made a point of working with independent food makers and artisans, and to promote and showcase their work as much as we do our own. And that's why we were pleased (but not surprised) at the enthusiasm and willingness of everyone

we reached out to when it came to creating never-before-seen culinary collaborations specifically for this chapter.

And by the way, paving the way for ourselves has never yielded as much as when we're paving the way for others to succeed alongside us. Looking back nearly a decade later, it is wonderful to see how many thriving businesses got their start here.

PG: Squid pro quo.

Paulie's Playlist

"The Coffee Song," Frank Sinatra

"Algo Más," Natalia Jiménez

"Bourbon Street Blues," Louis Prima

"It Takes Two," Marvin Gaye and
Kim Weston

"Mary Had a Little Lamb," Stevie
Ray Vaughan

"Green Onions," Booker T. and the
M.G.'s

"Goodbye Porkpie Hat," Jeff Beck

"I Love Lucy," Desi Arnaz

"Cut the Cake," Average White Band

"People," Arturo Sandoval and
Stevie Wonder

THE PARTNERS

ANDREW BELLUCCI'S PIZZERIA, QUEENS, NY

MG: Andrew Bellucci was pizza royalty, one of the absolute master pizzaiolos of NYC. When Paulie and I met him during one of our dinners away from the business, we immediately developed a wonderful friendship. He was the consummate professional and happiest when serving others and witnessing their enjoyment of his amazing food. Paulie and I miss him immensely. Since his passing, his partner, Matthew Katakis, has made sure that Andrew's legacy, recipes, and namesake restaurant live on.

AUNTS ET UNCLES, BROOKLYN, NY

MG: We met Mike and Nicole a few years ago when they came into our restaurant. They own a fabulous vegan shop in Flatbush and wanted to try our vegan pizza. Clearly they liked it because they've come back again and again, and we've returned the favor by frequenting Aunts et Uncles. This shop and café is actually not that far from where Paulie grew up. It's so welcoming. They totally embrace their Caribbean culture and roots and love to showcase their own unique style. And owners Mike and Nicole don't just serve vegan food, but their own merchandise and books as well. We find them truly inspiring.

BROOKLYN WHISKERS BAKERY, BROOKLYN, NY

MG: Brooklyn Whiskers is a feline-obsessed vegan café turned online bakeshop. Like me and Paulie, they created their brand on collaboration, carefully crafting relationships with other passionate makers, building something from nothing with like-minded artisans.

COMPTON'S, BROOKLYN, NY

Jimmy Collins, Co-Owner of Compton's: When Compton's opened in Greenpoint, we discovered a sense of community and a small-town feeling, and so much of that warmth came from our neighbors down the block at Paulie Gee's. The restaurant is a Greenpoint staple, and whether you're dining in or walking by Paulie and Mary Ann on the street, they make you feel at home!

EDITH'S SANDWICH COUNTER, BROOKLYN, NY

Elyssa Heller, Founder & CEO of Edith's: As a thank-you to Paulie Gee for using their space (see page 164), I began selling a signature Hellboy twist on the pizza bagel during pop-ups. I also sell it during our shop's anniversary week in August to celebrate getting my start in the back of 60 Greenpoint.

GREENPOT, BROOKLYN, NY

Ania Park and Magda Doroszkiewicz, Cofounders of GreenPot: We used to come by to eat pizza at the Paulie Gee's restaurant. We met Paulie first. He was always very welcoming and friendly with the guests. After opening our vegan place, we finally met Mary Ann. It is always such a pleasure to see Mrs. Gee. We love hearing about her experiences, and it feels nice to share stories. That connection and friendship is priceless from people as nice as Mrs. Gee and her husband.

LEROY'S, BROOKLYN, NY

MG: We met Chad out of necessity. Paulie needed some good Cuban pork for a Cuban sandwich pizza he planned to make for an event in Upstate New York. The pork we get from Federoff's is delicious, but not Cuban, and so we had to scramble to find another local source.

Bobby Little and Chad Urban, Chef/Owners of Leroy's: We love to collaborate with pioneers in the neighborhood and hope to continue well into the future!

PANZÓN, BROOKLYN, NY

David Taft and Nicole Onisick, Cofounders of Panzón: Our crew first met Paulie and Mary Ann when they came into Panzón on a warm summer day. There was a buzz throughout the restaurant as guests and staff spotted these local Greenpoint celebrities in our presence! We sat down with Paulie and Mary Ann to thank them for popping in, which then turned into a lengthy conversation as they offered us kindness, advice, and mentorship in the neighborhood.

VAN LEEUWEN, BROOKLYN, NY

Laura O'Neill, Cofounder of Van Leeuwen: We first met Paulie and Mary Ann through the Haslegrave brothers, who were simultaneously building out both of our very first locations. And it was clear that the Gees were as obsessed with pizza as we were with ice cream! It's been inspiring to witness the Paulie Gee's journey, and we continue to be proud to see our ice cream on their menu.

WHEATED, BROOKLYN, NY

MG: In 2010, David Sheridan was an amateur pizza maker working a marketing job. When the company downsized, he decided to realize his dream of starting a restaurant. Inspired by his family and with the support of his wife, he opened Wheated in 2013 to share his love for pizza and whiskey. Sound familiar?

PG: Well, other than the whiskey part.

David Sheridan, Founder of Wheated: I'm forever thankful to Paulie and Mary Ann for their mentorship and friendship. I've told them on several occasions that the longest-lasting impact of Paulie Gee's will be the folks who've come through its doors and gone on to do their own thing.

SFINGE

Makes 15 to 20 sfinge

We used to serve pie (not the pizza kind) at the restaurant, finished with apple cider caramel sauce and ricotta dollops. Here's that sauce, with a recipe for sfinge (which loosely translates to "ricotta balls") from David Sheridan (see page 161). —MG

- -

For the Apple Cider Caramel Sauce

2 cups apple cider

1 cup plus 2 tablespoons sugar

¼ cup light corn syrup

6 tablespoons heavy cream

¼ teaspoon ground cinnamon

½ teaspoon fine sea salt

For the Sfinge

4 to 6 cups neutral oil, such as canola or avocado oil, for frying

3 large eggs

½ cup sugar

1¾ cups (16 ounces) whole-milk ricotta cheese

2¼ cups self-rising cake flour, such as Presto

Make the sauce: In a medium pot, bring the cider to a boil over high heat. Reduce the heat to medium-low and simmer, stirring frequently, until the liquid has reduced by half, about 40 minutes.

Add the sugar, corn syrup, cream, cinnamon, and salt and cook, stirring frequently, until reduced by half, about 30 minutes. Remove from the heat and let sit at room temperature until ready to serve. You can heat it up briefly on the stovetop again if the sauce gets too thick and stiff.

Make the sfinge: Fill a deep fryer with oil or pour enough oil into a heavy-bottomed pot to fill it halfway. Heat the oil over medium-high heat until it registers 370°F on a deep-fry thermometer.

In a large bowl, whisk together the eggs and sugar until combined. Fold in the ricotta, then add the flour a little bit at a time, mixing continuously until everything is well incorporated.

Working in batches, use an ice cream scoop to drop tablespoons of the batter into the hot oil. Fry, using a slotted spoon to turn the sfinge as needed so all sides brown evenly, until golden brown, about 3 minutes. Transfer to a paper towel–lined plate to drain and repeat with the remaining batter, allowing the oil to return to 370°F between batches.

Serve the sfinge drizzled with the apple cider caramel sauce.

HELLBOY PIZZA BAGEL

Makes 1 pizza bagel

MG: Edith's started in August 2020 in the back of Paulie Gee's in Greenpoint. Founder Elyssa Heller had the idea of using a pizzeria during the day to make her signature hand-twisted wood-fired sourdough bagels. She knew she needed ovens that would go over 600°F.

PG: Being a Jewish Italian American (also known as a pizza bagel), this idea was exciting to me. Both bagels and pizza hold a special place in my heart.

• •

1 sesame bagel, sliced in half

3 ounces fresh whole-milk mozzarella cheese, sliced

½ cup Vegan Tomato Sauce (see page 91)

Grated Pecorino Romano cheese, for sprinkling

6 slices pepperoni or soppressata

Hot honey, for drizzling (we use Mike's)

Preheat the oven to 500°F. Line a baking sheet with parchment paper.

Set the bagel halves on the prepared baking sheet, cut-sides up. Layer the ingredients on the bagel halves in this order: mozzarella, sauce, a sprinkle of pecorino, pepperoni. Bake for 6 to 8 minutes, until the bagel is golden and the cheese has melted. Drizzle hot honey on top and enjoy!

NOTE

Once cooled, pizza bagels can be wrapped in plastic wrap and stored in the fridge for up to 3 days. They can also be wrapped in a wet paper towel, placed in a freezer-safe bag, and frozen for up to 6 months. Either refrigerated or frozen, they can be reheated the same way you originally baked them.

VANILLA-LIMONCELLO "CREAMSICLE"

Makes 1 quart each of vanilla
ice cream and lemon granita

When Van Leeuwen's vanilla ice cream (which we carry at the restaurant) meets our own lemon granita (inspired by my limoncello obsession), you get a next-level version of a Creamsicle. This would look lovely in sundae glasses or any sort of pretty bowl. —PG

· ·

For the Ice Cream

2 cups heavy cream

1 cup whole milk

½ cup plus 2 tablespoons sugar

¼ teaspoon kosher salt

1 plump vanilla bean, split in half lengthwise

8 large egg yolks

For the Granita

Zest of 1 lemon

1 cup fresh lemon juice (from 5 to 7 lemons)

1½ cups sugar

Paulie Gee's Homemade Limoncello (page 217), for serving (optional)

Make the ice cream: Pour the cream and milk into a double boiler or a heatproof bowl set over a pot of gently simmering water (the bottom of the bowl should not touch the water). Whisk in ½ cup of the sugar and the salt, then scrape the vanilla seeds into the pot and add the pod as well. Cook, stirring, until the sugar has dissolved and you see steam rising from the top. Remove from the heat, cover, and let the mixture steep for 15 minutes. Remove the vanilla bean pod.

Meanwhile, fill a large heatproof bowl with ice and water and set another bowl over it.

In a medium bowl, whisk together the egg yolks and remaining 2 tablespoons sugar until uniform. While whisking continuously, add a splash of the dairy mixture to the yolks and whisk to incorporate. Continue whisking in the dairy mixture, bit by bit, until you've added about half of it. (This prevents your yolks from scrambling!)

Pour the yolk mixture into the double boiler or bowl with the remaining dairy mixture. Cook over medium-low heat, stirring continuously with a wooden spoon, until steam begins to rise from the surface and the custard thickens enough to coat the back of the spoon. To test, hold your spoon horizontally and run your finger through the custard on the back. If the gap your finger leaves stays separated, the custard is ready.

Recipe continues

Pour the custard through a fine-mesh strainer into the bowl over the ice bath and stir until the custard has cooled, 3 to 5 minutes. Transfer the custard to a quart-size container, cover, and refrigerate for at least 4 hours or preferably overnight before churning.

Pour the custard into an ice cream maker and churn according to the manufacturer's instructions until the texture of the ice cream resembles soft serve. Transfer the ice cream back to the storage container and freeze to harden. (Alternatively, you can serve it immediately—it will have the consistency of gelato.)

Make the granita: In a small saucepan, combine the lemon zest, lemon juice, sugar, and 1¼ cups water and bring to a boil over high heat, stirring until the sugar has dissolved. Remove from the heat and let cool. Pour the mixture into a shallow metal baking pan, about 9×13 inches, give it a quick stir, and place the pan on a flat surface in the freezer.

After about 2 hours, stir the mixture with a fork, especially around the edges where it freezes faster, then put it back in the freezer. After another hour, repeat. The mixture should start coming together, looking more like a slushie. Return the granita to the freezer for another hour after fluffing with a fork. This process should take 5 to 6 hours in total. The finished granita should be an icy mixture throughout, without any liquid. Fluff once more with a fork before serving.

To serve, place a scoop of ice cream and a scoop of granita in each bowl, drizzle with limoncello, if desired, and enjoy.

BLOGGERS: THE FIRST INFLUENCERS

We can't talk about the people who helped us get where we are without bringing bloggers into the conversation. I started out as a casual fan of Adam Kuban—the original pizza blogger—and his blog, *Slice*. I'd leave comments on the message boards, always signing off as "Paulie Gee" instead of using my real name. So that's how that started.

After I built the oven, I began sharing pictures on Adam's site, all with the goal of getting him to participate in one of my NJ pizza tastings without me begging. I managed to catch the attention of writer Josh Levin first, after Adam reposted his article entitled "Pizza Oven Lifestyles—Episode 1." It told the story of a chile farmer with a wood-fired pizza oven on his property that he kept going constantly to feed the workers and his family. At the end of the article, Josh wrote, "If you know anyone who has a pizza-oven lifestyle, please contact me."

Well, I immediately sent links to pictures of my backyard pizza oven, along with the note, "Josh, we gotta tawk." Within a day, I'd arranged for Josh and his family to attend a pizza tasting. I think it goes without saying that it was a very enjoyable experience. And Josh wrote a glowing article about it, which Adam once again reposted.

Having landed on Adam's radar, I was able to get him out for that coveted tasting the day before Easter 2009. Not only that, but he brought Scott Wiener of Scott's Pizza Tours, as well as other top writers of the time, such as Alexandra Penfold (*Blondie & Brownie*) and Lois Heyman of Central Jersey's *Courier-News*. Adam even chronicled the evening with a piece called "An Evening with Paulie Gee, Pizza Madman."

Those are only a few of our first early "gets"—influential bloggers who became fans, then friends, and in some cases, even colleagues. And we're fortunate to remain close with all of them to this day. Our dear friend and *Slice* contributor, Mark Horowitz, passed away in 2024, and we're so happy a picture of him is featured here. **—PG**

CALZONE FRITTO "MAGIA BIANCA"

Makes 1 calzone

Paulie and I never look at other pizza makers as competition. Developing relationships with greats like Andrew Bellucci (see page 160) has always been important to us, because they understand the business like no one else does, and love it the way we do, despite all the ups and downs. Andrew was the consummate professional, and happiest when serving others enjoying his amazing food. He passed away in 2023, and Paulie and I miss him immensely. We're grateful to his partner for sharing a recipe inspired by our joint passion for pizza and our friendship, and hope to help his legacy live on in this book. —MG

• •

4 cups canola oil or vegetable oil, for frying

1 round NY-Style Dough (page 22) or your favorite pizza dough (about ½ pound)

4 ounces fresh whole-milk mozzarella cheese, sliced

4 ounces aged mozzarella cheese, sliced

4 ounces provolone cheese, sliced (about ½ cup)

¼ cup whole-milk ricotta cheese

¼ cup finely grated Pecorino Romano cheese, plus more for serving

Extra-virgin olive oil, for drizzling

Fine sea salt and freshly ground black pepper

Fines herbes (or a mix of equal parts chopped fresh parsley, chives, tarragon, and chervil), for sprinkling

½ cup Sake Pink Sauce (see page 73) or your favorite sauce, for dipping

Heat the oil in a deep fryer or a wide, heavy-bottomed pot over medium-high heat to 350°F.

Shape the dough into a round as you would for a small pie. Once the dough is stretched out, place the fresh mozzarella, aged mozzarella, provolone, ricotta, and pecorino over one half of the dough, leaving the other half exposed. Drizzle with olive oil and sprinkle with salt, pepper, and fines herbes to taste.

Fold the exposed half of the dough over the filled half and use a fork or spoon to seal the edges. Make sure the calzone is completely sealed so none of the filling comes out in the fryer.

Carefully place the calzone in the hot oil and fry until golden brown, 3 to 4 minutes (see Note). Lift the deep fryer basket out of the oil and let the calzone rest in the basket for a minute so the oil drips off. Transfer the calzone to a plate and garnish with a dusting of fines herbes and pecorino. Serve with the sake pink sauce on the side for dipping.

NOTE

Calzones can also be baked in a 550°F oven (or the hottest it gets) for 8 to 10 minutes instead of fried.

PAULIE'S VEGAN LIMONCELLO BLONDIES

Makes 12 blondies

When Brooklyn Whiskers Bakery owners Preesa and Michael moved to Greenpoint from Seattle, they were in search of the best vegan 'za in the land. I'm glad to know they considered ours it! They come to the restaurant for date nights, they bring out-of-town guests . . . and it was easy for us to return that loyalty by adding their incredible vegan desserts to our menu board. —MG

For the Blondies

2 cups soy milk

½ cup Paulie Gee's Homemade Limoncello (page 217)

2 tablespoons flaxseed meal

5 tablespoons hot water

1½ cups vegan margarine

3 cups packed light brown sugar

1 cup granulated sugar

1 teaspoon kosher salt

Zest and juice of 2 lemons

1 tablespoon pure vanilla extract

4 cups all-purpose flour

For the Limoncello Glaze

4 cups sifted powdered sugar

2 tablespoons Paulie Gee's Homemade Limoncello (page 217)

1 tablespoon pure maple syrup

1 teaspoon kosher salt

1 teaspoon pure vanilla extract

Pinch of ground turmeric, for color

Hot water, for thinning

Make the blondies: Preheat the oven to 350°F. Line a 9 × 13-inch cake pan with parchment paper.

In a small bowl, whisk together the soy milk and the limoncello. In another small bowl, mix the flaxseed meal with the hot water.

In a small saucepan, melt the margarine over medium-low heat.

In a medium bowl, whisk together the brown sugar, granulated sugar, salt, soy milk mixture, lemon zest, and lemon juice, followed by the flax mixture and the vanilla. Whisk in the melted margarine, followed by the flour, and mix until you see no lumps.

Pour the batter into the prepared pan. Bake for 40 minutes, until a toothpick inserted into the center comes out clean, rotating the pan halfway through. Remove from the oven and let cool.

Meanwhile, make the limoncello glaze: In a large bowl, whisk together the powdered sugar, limoncello, maple syrup, salt, vanilla, and turmeric to combine. Slowly whisk in hot water 1 tablespoon at a time until the glaze is thick but spreadable.

Cut the blondies into twelve 3 × 3¼-inch squares and use a spatula to carefully remove them from the pan. Use a spoon to drizzle the glaze over the top and let stand until the glaze just begins to harden before serving. Store any leftovers in an airtight container in the fridge for up to 5 days.

THE RICKY RICOTTA SANDWICH

Compton's makes sandwiches bigger and better. So what better inspiration than our popular Ricky Ricotta pie? Sausage, ricotta, and tomatoes (especially summer heirlooms) are as delicious layered between bread as they are on top of pizza crust. Almost. —MG

Makes 1 sandwich

· ·

2 (5-inch) sweet Italian sausage links, cut into ½-inch-thick slices

½ heirloom tomato, cut into ½-inch chunks

¼ cup chopped Vidalia onion

Semolina hero roll, cut in half lengthwise

Extra-virgin olive oil, for drizzling

½ cup whole-milk ricotta cheese

½ cup arugula

2 tablespoons Parmigiano Reggiano cheese, for sprinkling

In a large pan, cook the sausage over medium heat until some of the fat renders, about 5 minutes. Add the tomato and onion and cook until the sausage is cooked through and the tomato and onion are soft, about 5 minutes more.

Toast the hero roll cut-side up under the broiler or in a toaster oven until golden brown. Drizzle the toasted roll with olive oil and spread about a quarter of the ricotta on each cut side, reserving the rest to finish the sandwich. Add the arugula to one side of the roll and top with the sausage and vegetables from the pan. Sprinkle with the Parmigiano, finish with a few extra dollops of ricotta, and serve!

AJO MOJO PORK

Serves 10 or more

My daughter-in-law says this pork tastes just like her Cuban grandmother used to make it. So that is a great compliment. —MG

■■

5 pounds boneless pork shoulder

½ cup Dijon mustard

¼ cup Calabrian chile flakes, or 1 tablespoon red pepper flakes

1 tablespoon ground coriander

4½ teaspoons ground cumin

1½ teaspoons dried oregano

8 garlic cloves, crushed

¼ cup kosher salt, plus more as needed

2 cups chicken stock (not low-sodium)

2 limes, cut in half

3 oranges, cut in half

Your choice of one or more of the below, for serving:
Broccoli Rabe Pesto (see page 51)

Braised Fennel (see page 58)

Pickled Red Onions (see page 46)

Place the pork shoulder on a baking sheet. Rub with the mustard, chile flakes, coriander, cumin, and oregano and place in the fridge to marinate overnight.

The next day, preheat the oven to 300°F.

Place the garlic, salt, and stock in a deep roasting pan and set the pork shoulder on top. Squeeze the juice from the lime and orange halves into the pan, then place the juiced fruit into the pan as well. Cover the pan with aluminum foil. Place in the oven and cook for 3½ to 4½ hours, until the pork is tender and shreds easily with a fork. Remove the pork from the pan and let cool to room temperature.

Meanwhile, remove and discard the citrus from the pan, then pour all the liquid from the pan into a medium saucepan. Cook over medium-low heat until the liquid has reduced by about a third, about 10 minutes. Return the pork to the roasting pan along with the reduced liquid. Gently shred the pork with two forks and fold together with the liquid. Taste and adjust the seasoning to your liking.

Enjoy the shredded pork with any combo of pesto, fennel, and pickled onions, or see the note to take things up a notch.

NOTE

Optional: Line a large baking pan with plastic wrap. Place the shredded pork inside, smooth the top, then cover with parchment and a baking sheet. Place weights such as tomato cans on top. Refrigerate overnight in the fridge, then cut the pork into shapes (squares, triangles, etc.). Bread with flour, then beaten egg, then panko, and fry until golden brown, about 3 minutes per side, before serving with pesto, fennel, and/or onions.

VEGAN MEATLOAF
WITH PG TOMATO GLAZE

Serves 6

I met Ania and Magda (twin sisters who I still get mixed up) when they opened GreenPot, a vegan café and grocery in Greenpoint, during the COVID-19 pandemic. It was a god-send for the neighborhood vegans, who were all of a sudden compelled to do a lot more cooking at home. The Paulie Gee's team is always looking to grow our chops when it comes to vegan menu items. I'd say we nailed it on our vegan sausage, but this vegan meatloaf shows we can still learn a thing or two. —MG

....

½ cup walnuts

¼ cup pecans

¾ cup rolled oats

1 tablespoon flaxseed meal

1 tablespoon olive oil

1 medium onion, chopped (about 1 cup)

2 garlic cloves, chopped

1½ cups cremini mushrooms, diced

1 tablespoon dried Italian herbs

½ teaspoon kosher salt

½ teaspoon freshly ground black pepper

1 teaspoon chile powder

1 tablespoon Worcestershire sauce

1 cup cooked lentils

½ cup grated vegan Parmesan

2 tablespoons chopped fresh flat-leaf parsley

½ cup Vegan Tomato Sauce (see page 91), for glazing

Preheat the oven to 350°F. Line a 9 × 5-inch loaf pan with parchment paper.

In a food processor, combine the walnuts, pecans, and oats and process until crumbly (more fine than coarse, but not too fine).

Place the flaxseed meal in a small bowl and pour over 2 tablespoons water to create a "flax egg."

In a medium saucepan, heat the olive oil over medium heat. Add the onion and cook, stirring occasionally, for 1 minute, then add the garlic and cook for another minute. Add the mushrooms, Italian herbs, salt, pepper, chile powder, and Worcestershire. Cook, stirring occasionally, until the mushrooms soften, about 3 minutes.

In a large bowl, combine the nut mixture, sautéed mushrooms, flax egg, cooked lentils, Parmesan, and parsley. Gently fold together to combine. Place the mixture in the prepared loaf pan. Bake for 30 minutes. Glaze the top of the loaf with the tomato sauce, then bake for 10 minutes more, until fully cooked through and golden brown. Remove from the oven and serve.

LAMB BARBACOA
WITH FRENCH ONION SOUP

Serves 6 to 8

This dish is really a feast, and I can imagine making it for one of our dinner parties at home. I love the communal nature of it; it invites everyone to sit around a table together, make their own tacos, and, ideally, raise a drink like our Red Hot Madre Paloma (page 228) alongside! —MG

. . . .

For the Barbacoa

2 pounds boneless lamb shoulder roast

Kosher salt

4 garlic cloves, peeled

1 cup dried chickpeas

3 chiles de árbol

2 dried avocado leaves (see Note)

4 cups onion broth from French Onion Soup (page 152)

For Serving

Tortillas

Neutral oil, such as canola or avocado oil

Fresh cilantro

1 white onion, diced

Lime wedges

Your favorite salsa

NOTE

You can find dried avocado leaves at Mexican grocery stores or online, but bay leaves are an acceptable substitute.

Make the barbacoa: If the roast is tied, remove the string or netting. Salt the lamb liberally at least 1 hour before cooking. Preheat the oven to 275°F.

In a large Dutch oven or oven-safe pot, combine the lamb, garlic, chickpeas, chiles de árbol, and avocado leaves. Add enough water to make sure everything is submerged. Cover the pot, place in the oven, and cook for 6 hours, or until the internal temperature of the lamb registers 145°F.

Transfer the lamb from the pot to a platter to rest. Use a slotted spoon to transfer the chickpeas to another plate and set aside. Leave the liquid, avocado leaves, and chiles in the pot.

Add the onion broth to the pot and bring to a boil over high heat. Reduce the heat to maintain a simmer and cook for 30 minutes, until the liquid has reduced by one-quarter.

In a large pan, heat the tortillas in a drizzle of oil over medium-high heat. Strain the consommé, discarding the avocado leaves and chiles, and add the chickpeas to the consommé. Transfer to a ceramic dish. Shred the lamb on the platter using two forks. Place the dish of chickpeas to the side of the platter with the lamb. Garnish the lamb with cilantro and the onion, and serve with the tortillas, lime wedges, and salsa on the side for making little tacos or eating/dipping as desired.

ALL GREEN EVERYTHING

Serves 4 to 6

Mike and Nicole are another example of business owners who became customers who became collaborators and friends. They own Aunts et Uncles, a fabulous vegan restaurant in Flatbush, which isn't that far from where Paulie grew up. They totally embrace their culture and roots and love to showcase in their own unique style. We find them truly inspiring, and are honored to know they think the same of us. The recipe they created to embody our brand is about using only the best—no substitutes. —MG

⅓ cup olive oil (extra-virgin not necessary)

1 bunch asparagus, ends trimmed

12 Brussels sprouts, halved

12 ounces whole okra pods, halved

3 garlic cloves, sliced

½ teaspoon freshly ground black pepper

¾ teaspoon lemon pepper

Kosher salt

1 cup Vegan Kale Pesto (see page 80)

Zest and juice of 1 lemon

In a large nonstick pan, heat the olive oil over medium-high heat until hot but not smoking. Add the asparagus, Brussels sprouts, and okra and sear for 4 minutes without stirring. Flip the vegetables over and cook until browned and charred on the other side, a few minutes more.

Add the garlic, black pepper, lemon pepper, and salt to taste. Cook until the vegetables are tender and charred but not burnt, about 5 minutes more.

Transfer to a platter and top with the pesto and the lemon zest and juice. Enjoy!

CHAPTER SEVEN

HOME SLICE

"You learn something new every day, whether you want to or not."

PG: I love to cook, and I love to cook Italian food. My mother used to cook Italian food, which, being an Ashkenazi Jew, you'd think it wouldn't be so hot.

MG: She was a very good Italian cook. Also, his father used to cook, too.

PG: Yes, that's very important. At that time, Italian American men didn't cook. They barbecued maybe, sometimes, but otherwise, cooking was for a woman to do. Fairly early, at the age of around sixty-two, my father retired while my mom was still working. And so my mother said, "If I'm going to be working all day, I'm not about to cook when I come home." And that's when my dad took on that duty, which was a green light for me. If my father was willing to cook, maybe I could do it, too.

Cooking was like a liberation. It gave me the opportunity to make exactly what I wanted to eat. And getting married became another green light. We started cooking good stuff every night of the week. I had this great cookbook, Ada Boni's *Italian Regional Cooking*, that I used for inspiration. I think Mary Ann sold it.

MG: I always get blamed for everything.

PG: At a garage sale. She also sold my friend's grandfather's left-handed golf clubs. Anyway. Not only did we cook for ourselves, but we cooked for other people. Ten people at a time. Fifty for our annual Christmas party. I loved the chance to have people over.

MG: And believe me, they loved comin'. Being in our restaurants is really like an extension of being a guest in our home. We invite you in, you get to feel taken care of, and you eat delicious food. And while we can't invite everyone to one of those parties, you can use our family recipes to re-create a night at our place in your own home.

Paulie's Playlist

....

"Going to the Country," Steve Miller
Band

"The Country Life," The Silver Seas

"Country Comforts," Rod Stewart

"Country Road," James Taylor

"Country Pie," Bob Dylan

"House in the Country," Blood,
Sweat & Tears

"Valdez in the Country," Donny
Hathaway

"In the Country," Chicago

"Country Girl," Crosby, Stills,
Nash & Young

PAULIE'S ALL' AMATRICIANA

I adapted this recipe from my favorite Italian cookbook, *Italian Regional Cooking* by Ada Boni. But just a reminder here about how I use salt: I pretty much don't. I prefer to let salted butter and salted pasta water and salty cheese do the talking. But it's your house and your dinner. So if you must, add salt to taste. I just don't wanna know about it. —**PG**

Serves 4 to 6

1 (28-ounce) can whole peeled Italian-style tomatoes (not pureed or crushed), with their liquid

⅓ pound hickory smoked bacon (low-salt, if possible), chopped into small dice

1 medium sweet onion, chopped (about 1½ cups)

4 tablespoons (½ stick) salted butter

1 cup dry white wine

1 pound perciatelli or rigatoni

Fine sea salt

Grated Pecorino Romano cheese, for serving

Place the tomatoes and their liquid in a blender and puree. Pour the puree into a medium saucepan and cook over medium-low heat, stirring occasionally.

Meanwhile, in a second medium saucepan, cook the bacon over medium heat until the fat has rendered, about 3 minutes. Add the onion and cook, stirring occasionally to prevent the mixture from sticking to the bottom of the pot, until the mixture begins to turn golden brown, about 5 minutes. Add the butter and cook, stirring, until the mixture has turned fully golden brown, 5 minutes or so more. Add the wine and cook, stirring occasionally, until the alcohol has cooked out and the mixture has thickened slightly, about 10 minutes. Transfer the mixture to the saucepan with the tomatoes and cook over medium-low heat, stirring occasionally, for about 45 minutes.

Meanwhile, bring a large pot of water to a boil over high heat and salt it generously. Add the pasta and cook until al dente, 10 to 12 minutes. Drain the pasta. Serve the sauce over the pasta, generously sprinkled with pecorino.

RIGATONI & BROCCOLI

Serves 4

I adapted this from the broccoli "a crudo" recipe in the Rome-Lazio section of Ada Boni's *Italian Regional Cooking*, by serving it over rigatoni and adding mozzarella—WHOLE-MILK mozzarella. Don't you dare ruin this dish by trying to make it low fat. And DO NOT add any form of grated cheese. —**PG**

• •

Fine sea salt

½ pound large rigatoni

½ cup olive oil (extra-virgin not necessary)

8 garlic cloves, peeled

1 broccoli head, divided into florets

1 cup dry white wine

8 ounces low-moisture whole-milk mozzarella cheese, diced

Bring a large pot of water to a boil over high heat and salt it generously. Add the pasta and cook until al dente, 10 to 12 minutes. Drain the pasta and return it to the pot until ready to use.

Meanwhile, once you've added the pasta to the boiling water, heat a large skillet over medium heat. Pour in ¼ cup of the olive oil. When the oil is shimmering, add the garlic and cook, stirring, until golden brown, about 3 minutes. Add the broccoli florets and the remaining ¼ cup olive oil and cook, stirring regularly, until the broccoli begins to soften and the florets start to brown, about 8 minutes. Add the wine and cook, stirring, until the alcohol cooks off, about 5 minutes.

Place the mozzarella in a large serving bowl and add the hot pasta, stirring vigorously. Add the broccoli mixture and stir until the cheese has fully melted, then serve.

JACK DANIEL'S PENNE

Serves 4 to 6

Paulie was looking for a way to make typical vodka sauce more interesting. And let's be honest, vodka itself doesn't bring a whole lot to the party. Jack Daniel's, on the other hand, with its smoky and spicy notes, is quite the party guest. —MG

· ·

1 (28-ounce) can whole peeled Italian-style tomatoes, drained

4 tablespoons olive oil (extra-virgin not necessary)

10 garlic cloves: 4 peeled but kept whole, 6 chopped

1 cup heavy cream

½ cup Jack Daniel's whiskey

Fine sea salt

1 pound penne rigate

NOTE

Grated cheese is ABSOLUTELY NOT called for on this dish. When you taste it, you will understand why.

Place the tomatoes in a blender and puree.

In a medium saucepan, heat 2 tablespoons of the olive oil over medium heat. Add the 4 whole garlic cloves and cook, stirring, until golden brown, about 3 minutes. Use a slotted spoon to remove the garlic cloves from the pan and discard. Reduce the heat to medium-low and add the pureed tomatoes. Cook, stirring occasionally, until you're ready to use the tomatoes, about 15 minutes.

Meanwhile, heat the remaining 2 tablespoons olive oil in a second medium saucepan over medium heat. Add the chopped garlic and cook, stirring, until golden brown, about 3 minutes. Reduce the heat to medium-low and add the cream and whiskey to the pan. Simmer, stirring regularly, until the alcohol has cooked off, about 10 minutes.

Add the whiskey-cream mixture to the pan of tomatoes and cook until slightly thickened, about 30 minutes.

Meanwhile, bring a large pot of water to a boil over high heat and salt it generously. Add the pasta and cook until al dente, 10 to 12 minutes. Drain the pasta, top with the sauce, and serve.

PENNE
WITH OVERNIGHT SAUCE

Serves 4 to 6

I read about this sauce in an article in some cooking magazine and decided to try it out for one of our summer BBQs. It works well because there's no reason to serve cooked sauce when it's already hot outside, and it's very simple to execute. Even Mrs. Gee has made it. Salt draws water out from the tomatoes, which condenses their flavor, just like cooking does. So I guess there is an occasional purpose for salt. —PG

• •

2 (28-ounce) cans whole peeled Italian-style tomatoes, drained

¼ cup olive oil (extra-virgin not necessary)

1 medium to large Vidalia or sweet onion, chopped (about 1½ cups)

½ cup chopped fresh basil

1½ teaspoons fine sea salt, plus more as needed

1 pound penne rigate (or your favorite pasta shape)

Freshly grated Pecorino Romano cheese, for serving

NOTE

Penne is just the tip of the iceberg. Use this sauce in any recipe that calls for a meatless tomato sauce.

Place the tomatoes in a blender and puree. Pour the tomatoes into a large nonreactive (i.e., glass or ceramic, not metal) bowl.

In a medium saucepan, heat the olive oil over medium heat. Add the onion and cook, stirring occasionally, until deep golden brown, about 8 minutes.

Add the sautéed onion to the bowl of tomatoes along with the basil and salt. Stir to combine. Cover the bowl with plastic wrap and let stand at room temperature overnight. Absolutely do not refrigerate.

The next day, bring a large pot of water to a boil over high heat and salt it generously. Add the pasta and cook until al dente, 10 to 12 minutes. Drain the pasta, ladle the sauce over the top, sprinkle with pecorino, and serve.

QUICK & EASY LINGUINE
WITH RED CLAM SAUCE

Serves 8 to 10 as a main course

This is a simple way to enjoy linguine and red clam sauce, so you don't have to spend a lot of money on fresh clams and a lot of time cleaning and cooking them. It also serves a lot, so it's a good choice for dinner parties. I know you've heard this before, but if you don't want to get on Paulie's bad side, please do not use grated cheese of any kind on this dish. —MG

¼ cup olive oil (extra-virgin not necessary)

8 garlic cloves, peeled

3 (28-ounce) cans whole peeled Italian-style tomatoes, drained

4 (6½-ounce) cans chopped (not minced) clams, juice from 3 cans reserved

Fine sea salt

1½ pounds linguine fini

In a large saucepan, heat the olive oil and garlic over medium heat until the garlic is golden brown, about 3 minutes. Use a slotted spoon to remove the garlic from the pan and discard. Turn off the heat.

Place one-third of the tomatoes in a blender. Pulse until pureed, then pour into the pan you cooked the garlic in. Repeat with the remaining tomatoes.

Add the reserved clam juice to the pan. Bring to a simmer over medium heat and cook until the sauce thickens, about 10 minutes. Add the clams to the pan and simmer for 4 minutes more, until the clams are heated through.

Meanwhile, bring a large pot of water to a boil over high heat and salt it generously. Add the pasta and cook until al dente, 8 to 10 minutes. Drain, place in a large bowl, top with the sauce, and serve.

STUFFED MUSHROOMS

This recipe came to us from a close family friend, Mary Catanzarita, and is her version of the classic appetizer. When shopping, try to pick a package that has as many small mushrooms as possible. They cook more quickly and are the perfect single bite. —MG

Serves 2 or 3 as an appetizer

¼ cup olive oil (extra-virgin not necessary), plus more for greasing

16 ounces whole cremini or button mushrooms

6 garlic cloves, peeled

½ cup fresh flat-leaf parsley leaves

1 cup plain breadcrumbs

¼ teaspoon table salt

¼ cup freshly grated Pecorino Romano cheese

3 lemons

Preheat the oven to 375°F. Lightly grease a baking sheet.

Remove the stems from the mushrooms and set the caps aside. Place the stems in a food processor along with the garlic and parsley. Process into a fine mixture.

Place the breadcrumbs in a large bowl and add the mushroom mixture, stirring vigorously. Add the salt, pecorino, olive oil, and the juice of 2 of the lemons and stir again until well mixed.

Stuff the mushroom caps with the mushroom mixture, making sure it's fully packed in. Place the mushrooms on the prepared baking sheet and bake for 15 to 20 minutes, until slightly browned on top. (Keep in mind that larger mushrooms may take longer.)

Slice the remaining lemon into quarters and place on a serving platter with the mushrooms. Squeeze a bit of lemon juice over the mushrooms just before eating.

Sun-Dried Tomato &
Gorgonzola Spread
(page 198)

Sweet Red Roasted
Pepper Sauté
(page 199)

GARLIC BREAD

Serves 4 to 6

This is Paulie's favorite way to prepare an Italian American classic. (Enjoyed at home, of course, since we don't do bread at the restaurants.) —MG

½ cup (1 stick) salted butter

½ cup extra-virgin olive oil

1 cup fresh flat-leaf parsley leaves

1½ large garlic heads, cloves separated and peeled

1 long, thin loaf of semolina bread, with or without seeds

Place the stick of butter in an extra-large coffee mug. Microwave on high until fully melted, about 1 minute. Add the olive oil to the mug and stir to combine.

In a food processor, coarsely chop the parsley and garlic, then add them to the mug. Mix vigorously with a spoon. Place the mug in the freezer for about 30 minutes or refrigerate overnight.

Forty-five minutes to an hour before you're ready to make the bread, take the butter mixture out of the freezer or refrigerator and let it come to room temperature.

Preheat the oven to 375°F.

Slice the bread into ½-inch-thick rounds and arrange them on a baking sheet. (A long, thin loaf should yield about 30 slices.) Spread the butter mixture on both sides of the bread slices. Bake for about 10 minutes, until the tops are golden brown. Serve.

SUN-DRIED TOMATO & GORGONZOLA SPREAD

Makes 2 cups

This is wonderful to serve with Garlic Bread (page 197) or toasted Italian bread slices. Always a hit! —MG

··

½ cup pine nuts (pignoli), toasted

¼ cup jarred sun-dried tomatoes marinated in olive oil

1 cup mascarpone cheese

¼ cup crumbled Gorgonzola cheese

Combine all the ingredients in a food processor and process until fully combined and a consistent light reddish-orange color. Transfer the spread to a small serving bowl and smooth out the top with a butter knife. Cover and refrigerate for at least 1 hour before serving. Leftovers can be stored in an airtight container in the fridge for up to 5 days.

SWEET RED ROASTED PEPPER SAUTÉ

Serves 4 as an appetizer

This is one of my personal favorite recipes of Paulie's. You can serve it as an appetizer over Garlic Bread (page 197), spooned over pork chops or steak, or in a sandwich when paired with sausage or braciole in a roll.

The only issue is that it's painstaking work to deal with the peppers, which is why, now that we're so busy in the hospitality industry, we haven't made it at home in quite some time. I do not want to discourage YOU from making it, though, because it is well worth the effort. You will not be disappointed! —MG

¼ cup olive oil (extra-virgin not necessary), plus more for grilling

2 pounds sweet red peppers

3 large portobello mushrooms, thickly sliced

8 garlic cloves, peeled

½ teaspoon fine sea salt

½ cup pine nuts (pignoli), toasted

Heat a grill to high or heat a grill pan over high heat. Lightly oil the whole peppers and the mushroom slices. Place the peppers and mushroom slices sideways on the grill grate and grill, using tongs to flip the mushroom slices once and to turn the peppers as needed to make sure each side is mostly charred but still retains some red color, about 6 minutes total.

Transfer the mushrooms to a plate and place the peppers inside a paper grocery bag. Close the bag tightly and let the peppers sit for 1 hour. Remove the skin and seeds from the peppers and slice into pieces roughly 2 inches by ½ inch. Be sure to remove ALL the seeds, or they'll add a bitter taste to your dish.

In a large skillet, heat the olive oil and the garlic over medium heat and cook, stirring, until the garlic just starts to turn golden, about 3 minutes. Use a slotted spoon to remove the garlic from the pan and discard. Reduce the heat to medium-low, add the roasted peppers and the salt, and cook, stirring occasionally, for about 10 minutes. Add the mushrooms and pine nuts and cook, stirring occasionally, for 1 minute more before serving. Leftovers can be stored in an airtight container in the fridge for up to 1 week.

FRIED RAVIOLI

Makes at least 12 ravioli

This was a mainstay for our annual Christmas Party. Paulie would be cooking for at least a week prior, and I always helped with some of the prep and shopping. Although, let's be honest, Paulie still did most of the shopping, as he has always been very particular about ingredients.

Weeks before the party, our guests would be asking if our fried ravioli was going to be served. We would tell them to make sure they arrived early, because as soon as we put out the trays, they were gone.

This is more of a method than a recipe. You'll want to make at least a dozen ravioli, and you can double, triple, or quadruple the recipe from there. Adjust the breading and frying ingredients based on how many ravioli you're using. —MG

- -

All-purpose flour (at least 1 cup)

Beaten eggs (1 for every 4 ravioli)

Plain breadcrumbs (at least 1 cup)

Fresh large cheese ravioli (at least 12)

Canola or vegetable oil (at least 2 cups)

Powdered sugar, for sprinkling

NOTE

If you can't find fresh ravioli, forget it and move on to another recipe.

Set out three shallow dishes. Add the flour to one, the beaten egg to the second, and the breadcrumbs to the third. Coat each ravioli with flour, then dip in the egg, and coat with plain breadcrumbs. Set on a baking sheet.

Line a tray with paper towels and set it near the stove. In a large saucepan or deep fryer, heat the oil over medium-high heat until it reaches somewhere between 325° and 375°F on a deep-fry thermometer. Using a slotted spoon, place a few ravioli at a time in the hot oil and fry until golden brown, using the spoon to flip the ravioli as needed so they brown on all sides. This shouldn't take more than a couple of minutes.

Use the slotted spoon to transfer the fried ravioli to the paper towel–lined tray and sprinkle with powdered sugar. Repeat with the remaining ravioli, allowing the oil to return to 325° to 375°F between batches. Serve immediately.

SHRIMP SCAMPI

Serves 6 to 8

NYC's Little Italy used to be a cool place to go to. Probably will be again. Anyway, there was this spot we visited on Kenmare Street about thirty years ago called Little Charlie's Clam Bar. And they had shrimp scampi on their menu.

I was never that into shrimp scampi before, never made it at home. But theirs was really special to me for this one reason: They hardly cooked their garlic at all. Just threw it in at the last minute. And that's how I started to do mine. It really makes all the difference.

Sometimes I'll make scampi over spaghetti fini for the staff to have at lunch before we open. Never pizza. What? . . . I'm going to have guests show up, look through the glass doors while they're waiting to come in, and look at all of these people eating pizza? **—PG**

Fine sea salt

1 pound thin spaghetti

12 garlic cloves, peeled

½ cup fresh flat-leaf parsley leaves

½ cup (1 stick) salted butter

½ cup olive oil (extra-virgin not necessary), plus more if needed

1 pound extra-large shrimp, peeled, tails removed, and deveined

Juice of 3 large or 5 small lemons, plus more for serving

Bring a large pot of water to a boil over high heat and salt it generously. Add the pasta and cook until al dente, 8 to 10 minutes. Drain the pasta and set aside.

Meanwhile, in a food processor, chop the garlic and the parsley and set aside. In a large skillet, melt the butter over medium heat, then add the olive oil. Add the shrimp and cook until the bottoms are pink, about 2 minutes. Turn the shrimp over and add the lemon juice. Reduce the heat to medium-low and cook until the shrimp are pink all the way through, about 3 minutes more. Before removing the pan from the heat, add the chopped garlic and parsley and give everything a quick stir.

Place the spaghetti in a large serving bowl and toss with the shrimp mixture. If it seems too dry, add some more olive oil. Add more lemon juice to taste and serve.

SPINACH SAUTÉ
WITH AMARETTI COOKIES

```
Serves 4 to 6
```

PG: I've always loved the contrast of sweet and savory. That's how I came up with this recipe for my son's middle school class cookbook. I named it Derek's Magic Spinach. Everyone who's had it loves it and asks for it.

MG: I don't care for cookies with the spinach. That's not my cup of tea.

PG: And that's why she's the administrative arm of the business.

- -

¼ cup olive oil (extra-virgin not necessary)

10 garlic cloves, smashed and peeled

2 (10-ounce) bags baby spinach leaves

Fine sea salt

12 hard amaretti cookies

NOTE

There's absolutely no substitute for amaretti cookies here, so you better go out and find them. No soft cookies, though; they have to be the hard crunchy ones. That's very important. Doria is a good brand, and they're available at Italian specialty food shops.

In a large skillet, heat the olive oil and garlic over medium heat until the garlic is fragrant and golden brown, about 2 minutes. Remove the garlic using a slotted spoon and discard.

Add the spinach to the hot oil (you might want to use a splatter guard for this step). Cook, stirring occasionally, until the spinach is wilted. Taste and season with salt.

Transfer the spinach to a large serving dish. Crumble half the cookies over the spinach and stir them in. Crumble the remaining cookies evenly over the spinach and serve.

PIZZA RUSTICA

Makes 24 appetizer-size squares

This recipe is from our dear friend's mom, Mary Catanzarita. She was part of our extended family, which is how we got access to the consummate Italian Easter dish, Pizza Rustica. Nothing like the kind of pies you'll find at our restaurant, it's more of an eggy tart, with meats and cheeses folded inside the crust. But don't save it for Easter—it's a great brunch dish to feed a crowd all year long. **—MG**

Butter, for greasing

6 ready-made pie crusts, such as Pillsbury refrigerated pie crusts

2 cheese-and-parsley sausage pinwheels (about 1 pound each; see Note)

5 large eggs

1½ pounds boiled ham, diced (about 4 cups)

2 pounds whole-milk ricotta cheese (about 3¾ cups)

1 cup grated Pecorino Romano cheese

1 cup chopped fresh flat-leaf parsley

NOTE

You can find cheese-and-parsley sausage pinwheels in the meat section of the grocery store or at the butcher's counter, especially in Italian stores. If you can't find them, choose whatever uncooked sausage looks good to you.

Preheat the oven to 400°F. Grease a 9 × 13-inch pan with butter, and line the bottom with 4 of the pie crusts. They should dangle halfway over the sides of the pan.

In a large pan or grill pan, cook the sausage pinwheels over high heat until seared or grill marks develop on all sides, about 1 minute per side. Transfer the pinwheels to a cutting board and cut them into ½-inch pieces.

In a large bowl, beat 4 of the eggs. Add the chopped sausage, ham, ricotta, pecorino, and parsley and stir well to combine.

Spread the mixture evenly in the prepared pan. Using a rolling pin, roll the remaining two crusts together so they are conjoined and cut them into a large rectangle. Place over the exposed filling so it's covered. Fold the half-moons of crust that are hanging over the pan on top of the rectangle so the rustica is encased by dough all around.

Pierce the crust several times with a fork and bake for 1 hour 15 minutes. You can cover the top with foil if it starts to brown before the time is up. Remove the pan from the oven. Beat the remaining egg in a bowl. Brush the top of the crust with the beaten egg and bake for about 5 minutes more, until the egg wash is cooked and shiny but not burnt. Remove the pan from the oven and let cool for 30 minutes before cutting and serving.

BAKED SHRIMP

Serves 2 or 3 as an
appetizer

There's something celebratory about shrimp. They always make a party feel special. We have our great friend and cook Mary Catanzarita to thank for this recipe as well, and I especially appreciate that it's baked and not fried. No one wants their kitchen covered in splattered oil just before guests arrive. —MG

Vegetable oil or cooking spray, for greasing

6 garlic cloves, peeled

½ cup fresh flat-leaf parsley leaves

1 cup plain breadcrumbs

¼ teaspoon fine sea salt

¼ cup olive oil (extra-virgin not necessary)

Juice of 2 lemons

½ pound extra-large shrimp, peeled, tails removed, and deveined

1 lemon, quartered

Preheat the oven to 375°F. Lightly grease a 13 × 18-inch baking sheet.

Place the garlic and parsley in a food processor and process into a fine mixture. Transfer to a large bowl and add the breadcrumbs. Stir vigorously with a rubber spatula to combine. Add the salt, olive oil, and lemon juice and stir until well mixed.

Add the shrimp to the bowl and toss gently using the spatula or your hands to make sure they're generously and evenly coated on all sides. Spread them out on the prepared baking sheet in a single layer and sprinkle with additional breading mixture from the bowl. Bake for 10 to 15 minutes, until lightly browned on top.

Transfer the shrimp to a serving platter and place the lemon quarters alongside. Squeeze some lemon juice on the shrimp just before eating.

CHICKEN
WITH VINEGAR PEPPERS & MUSHROOM SAUCE

Serves 4

We began adding this recipe to the rotation when we got tired of the typical Italian dishes like chicken Parm. Don't get me wrong, we love Parm. But when you run out of things to do with chicken, this is a great, flavorful option—one that doesn't require a ton of sauce and cheese. —MG

▪ ▪

For the Sauce

4 tablespoons (½ stick) salted butter

2 tablespoons all-purpose flour

2 cups chicken broth, plus more if needed

8 ounces sliced cremini or white button mushrooms

1 (12-ounce) jar marinated vinegar pepper strips

For the Chicken

2 large eggs, beaten

2 cups Italian breadcrumbs, such as 4C brand, plus more as needed

2 pounds boneless, skinless chicken cutlets, pounded thin

1 cup olive oil (extra-virgin not necessary), plus more as needed

Make the sauce: In a medium saucepan, melt the butter over low heat. Sprinkle in the flour and cook, stirring, to create a brown paste, about 1 minute. Add the broth and stir until the roux is completely combined and the raw flour taste is cooked out, about 2 minutes.

Increase the heat to medium and add the mushrooms. Stir to combine. Carefully drain the liquid from the jar of peppers into the pot (set the peppers aside to use later) and stir to combine. Bring to a boil, then reduce the heat to medium-low and simmer, stirring occasionally, until thickened, about 15 minutes. Reduce the heat to low and keep warm, stirring occasionally, until the chicken is ready. If the sauce thickens too much, you can stir a little more broth into the pot.

Make the chicken: Place the eggs in one wide, shallow bowl and breadcrumbs in another. Dip each cutlet thoroughly in the egg, then in the breadcrumbs, making sure all sides are evenly and completely coated. Set the coated cutlets on a baking sheet or plate.

In a large skillet, heat the olive oil over medium heat. Add as many chicken cutlets as will fit, working in batches if necessary. Cook until golden on the first side, about 4 minutes, then flip and cook until golden on the second side, about 4 minutes more. Transfer to a plate and repeat with the remaining cutlets, adding more oil to the pan between batches if needed.

Just before serving, stir the reserved marinated peppers into the pot of sauce. Heat for about 1 minute, until warmed through.

To serve, divide the chicken cutlets among four plates. Spoon liberal amounts of sauce over each cutlet and enjoy.

CRAWFISH MONICA

Serves 6 to 8

This recipe was inspired by one of the most popular dishes served at the New Orleans Jazz & Heritage Festival. The line at the Crawfish Monica booth is one of the longest on the fairgrounds. For gatherings both large and small, this simple and elegant dish will impress your guests in a big way. Serve this pasta with some nice French bread and a dry white wine. **—MG**

▪▪

½ cup (1 stick) unsalted butter

1 good-size bunch green onions, chopped

5 garlic cloves (to your taste), chopped

1 pound crawfish tails, boiled and peeled; OR 1 pound shrimp, peeled, tails removed and deveined; OR 1 pound lump crabmeat, drained, if needed; OR 1 pound oysters, drained and quartered

2 cups half-and-half

1 to 2 tablespoons Creole seasoning, or to taste

Fine sea salt

1 pound pasta (rotini is traditional, but use your favorite shape)

NOTE

If crawfish is not readily available in your area, this recipe works well with shrimp, oysters, or crabmeat.

In a large pot, melt the butter over medium heat. Add the green onions and garlic and cook, stirring, for 3 minutes. Add the seafood and cook for 2 minutes more.

Add the half-and-half and several big pinches of Creole seasoning, tasting the sauce before each pinch until the flavor is to your liking. Cook over medium heat, stirring often, until the sauce thickens, 5 to 10 minutes.

Meanwhile, bring a large pot of water to a boil over high heat and salt it generously. Add the pasta and cook until al dente, 10 to 12 minutes. Drain the pasta, add it to the pot with the sauce, and toss well to coat. Reduce the heat to low and cook, stirring often, for 10 minutes or so more. Serve immediately.

CHAPTER EIGHT

WHEN LIFE GIVES YOU LEMONS, MAKE LIMONCELLO

"We don't play background music, we play foreground music."

PG: We finally got a license to serve wine and beer six months after we opened. It really helped with sales but was challenging at first, because guests still tried to bring their own. It was better when we received our full liquor license. That allowed us to serve our house-made limoncello.

I started offering limoncello during our at-home pizza tastings, and it became a signature thing. I like handing it out right before the meal starts, when you're waiting for your food or waiting for a table. It has the tendency to make whatever you're eating taste a little better. And of course, it makes the whole dining experience a little better, too.

MG: We eventually came up with a full-blown cocktail menu. Like our salads and soups, preparing cocktails allows us to make good on a low-waste policy by using up the extra bits of this and that we always have in the restaurant. And cocktails are very "on brand" for Paulie, since they're essentially classics injected with his taste and personality.

PG: Now, *there's* a reason to drink.

Paulie's Playlist

■ ■

"Feel the Need in Me," Detroit Emeralds

"Pickleback," Ryan Anselmi

"Wicked Wine," Lee Ritenour

"Bottle of Red Wine," Eric Clapton

"Strawberry Wine," The Band

"Whiskey Train," Procol Harum

"Gin House Blues," Mike Mattison

PAULIE GEE'S HOMEMADE LIMONCELLO

Makes 1 liter (about 4 cups)

Limoncello is grain alcohol infused with lemon oil and mixed with simple syrup. Guests at our restaurants love celebrating a birthday or anniversary with this drink. Many have said it's the best they've ever had! **—MG**

. . . .

1 liter 190-proof grain alcohol, such as Everclear

Zest of 12 lemons

4½ cups sugar

Pour the grain alcohol into a 2-quart wide-mouth jar. Add the lemon zest and seal the jar. Place the jar in a cool place and let stand for 2 weeks, shaking or stirring the mixture every few days.

Fill a large pot with 5 cups water and add the sugar. Bring to a boil over high heat, then immediately reduce the heat to medium. Cook, stirring occasionally, until the sugar has completely dissolved and you're left with simple syrup, about 1 minute. Remove from the heat and let cool to room temperature.

Carefully pour the grain alcohol through a fine-mesh strainer into the pot of syrup and stir to combine; discard the lemon zest. Using a funnel, carefully distribute the limoncello among glass bottles and seal. Store at room temperature; it will keep indefinitely.

To serve, place a bottle of limoncello in the freezer at least 6 hours before you plan on using it, along with the glasses you intend to pour it into, and remove just before serving.

LIMONCELLO MARGARITA

Makes 1 drink

The opening bartender at the Philly location of our Slice Shop (see page 110) came up with this drink. Paulie liked it so much, we decided to bring it to Brooklyn. Thanks, Brenton! —MG

• •

2 ounces Paulie Gee's Homemade Limoncello (page 217), or store-bought

2 ounces Hornitos Plata silver tequila

2 ounces fresh lemon juice

Lemon wedge, for garnish

Combine the limoncello, tequila, and lemon juice in a cocktail shaker filled with ice. Shake to combine, then pour into a soda glass filled with ice. Garnish with the lemon wedge.

LIMONCELLO SPRITZER

Our limoncello is a hit every time of year, but turning it into a spritzer is a great way to lighten it up a bit for summer. And this is so easy to make in large batches for a party. —MG

Makes 1 drink

░░░

2 ounces Paulie Gee's Homemade Limoncello (page 217), or store-bought

Chilled club soda, for topping

Lemon wedge, for garnish

Pour the limoncello into a stemmed glass and top with club soda. Stir to combine and garnish with the lemon wedge.

GEE STING

Why bother with sugar or simple syrup? Using hot honey syrup in this classic drink is a no-brainer. And how about that name? It works on so many levels. —PG

Makes 1 drink

░░░

2 ounces Paulie Gee's Homemade Limoncello (page 217), or store-bought

Drizzle of hot honey syrup (see page 227)

Cold club soda, for topping

Lemon wedge, to garnish

Pour the limoncello and hot honey syrup into a stemmed glass and stir to combine. Top with club soda and garnish with the lemon wedge.

PAULIE COLADA

Makes 1 drink

Paulie may be the front man, but I'm taking credit for coming up with a piña colada that doesn't need a special slushy machine, or even a blender. —MG

- -

1½ ounces Malibu coconut-flavored rum

½ ounces Disaronno amaretto

4½ ounces pineapple juice

Maraschino cherry, for garnish

Combine the rum, amaretto, and pineapple juice in a cocktail shaker filled with ice. Shake to combine, then strain into a pint glass filled with ice. Garnish with the cherry.

PICKLEBACK MARTINI

Makes 1 drink

I love a good dirty martini. And I got turned on to picklebacks—whiskey followed by a shot of dill pickle juice—at Shayz Lounge, just around the corner from 60 Greenpoint. This drink is the best of all possible worlds. —PG

- -

3 ounces Tito's vodka

¾ ounce pickle juice (from a jar of pickles)

Pickle spear on a cocktail skewer, for garnish

Combine the vodka and pickle juice in a cocktail shaker filled with ice. Shake to combine, then strain into a chilled martini glass. Garnish with the pickle spear.

PICKLED PINEAPPLE MARTINI

Makes 1 drink

....

3 ounces Tito's vodka

¾ ounce juice from a jar of Pickled Pineapple (see page 49)

3 chunks of Pickled Pineapple (see page 49) on a cocktail skewer, for garnish

Combine the vodka and pickled pineapple juice in a cocktail shaker filled with ice. Shake to combine, then strain into a chilled martini glass. Garnish with the skewered pickled pineapple.

LILI & CATA ESPRESSO MARTINI

`Makes 1 drink`

Our neighbors and friends Lili and Jorge Rojas are the owners of a lovely nail salon with a coffee-wine bar called Lili & Cata attached. We didn't have an espresso machine in our shop, so we asked them if they'd like to provide us with the cold brew for this drink. They were happy to partner with us, and everyone benefited . . . guests definitely included! **—MG**

• •

1½ ounces Tito's vodka

1 ounce Kahlúa liqueur

1 ounce cold brew espresso

3 espresso beans, for garnish

Combine the vodka, Kahlúa, and cold brew in a cocktail shaker filled with ice. Shake to combine, then strain into a chilled martini glass. Garnish with the espresso beans.

MIKEY PALOMA

Makes 1 drink

The Hellboy (page 40) got Mike's Hot Honey to where it is, but we've found all sorts of ways to use the honey over the years, including in sundaes and cocktails. We used it make this particular drink in large batches for events in the early days of the business, before officially adding it to our opening cocktail menu. —**PG**

. . . .

½ cup Mike's Hot Honey

1½ ounces Hornitos Plata silver tequila

2 ounces fresh grapefruit juice

Club soda, for topping

Orange peel, for garnish

NOTE

You only need a drizzle of the hot honey syrup for this drink, but it will keep in an airtight container in the fridge for up to 1 month. Try it in the Gee Sting (page 220) or the Red Hot Madre Paloma (page 228).

In a small saucepan, combine the hot honey and ½ cup water and bring to a simmer over medium heat, stirring until the honey is dissolved. Remove from the heat and let cool before using.

Combine the tequila, grapefruit juice, and a drizzle of the hot honey syrup in a cocktail shaker filled with ice. Shake to combine, then strain into a rocks glass filled with ice. Top with club soda and garnish with the orange peel.

RED HOT MADRE PALOMA

Makes 1 drink

Technically, you can use any brand of mezcal you'd like. But Madre smokes their agave in an earthen pit, which is why their mezcal adds the perfect hint of smoke to go along with the spice in this cocktail. —MG

. . . .

1½ ounces Madre Mezcal

2 ounces fresh grapefruit juice

Splash of hot honey syrup
(see page 227)

Club soda, for topping

Lime wedges, for garnish

Combine the mezcal, grapefruit juice, and hot honey syrup in a cocktail shaker filled with ice. Shake to combine, then strain into a highball glass filled with ice. Top with club soda and garnish with the lime wedges.

PAULIE NEGRONI

Makes 1 drink

PG: I like Negronis, but have always found Campari a little too bitter. Well, one night in our Philly Slice Shop (see page 110), they ran out of Campari and started using Aperol in their Negronis instead. I loved it, because not only is it less bitter, it's a lot lighter. And our guests can't get enough of it on tap.

MG: As far as the name goes, some naysayers will tell you there's already an Aperol-based Negroni called the Contessa. But Paulie is ignoring that possible fact.

· ·

1 ounce Beefeater gin

1 ounce Aperol

1 ounce sweet vermouth

Orange peel, for garnish

Combine the gin, Aperol, and vermouth in a cocktail shaker filled with ice. Shake to combine, then strain into a rocks glass filled with ice. Garnish with the orange peel.

CHAPTER NINE

SWEET TREATS

"Having no room is no excuse for not eating."

There's so much more to hospitality than the main course. Desserts may come at the end of a meal, but they shouldn't be an after-thought. They play just as important a role in setting the scene.

You know that I only serve what I love. So what you'll never find me making is a Nutella pizza. It's such a cliché, and don't ever ask me to do something that's a cliché. As for Mary Ann, well, she is the queen of sweets in our house. Except nothing is as sweet as her. **—PG**

Paulie's Playlist

"Los Conquistadores Chocolatés," Johnny Hammond

"Cherry Pie," Sade

"Squib Cakes," Tower of Power

"Sugar Pie Guy," The Joneses

"Feel the Need in Me," Detroit Emeralds

"Ice Cream Cakes," Jeff Beck Group

"Little Green Apples," O.C. Smith

"Sugar Sugar," Wilson Pickett

"I Can't Help Myself (Sugar Pie Honey Bunch)," Four Tops

"How Sweet It Is to Be Loved by You," Marvin Gaye

"A Marshmallow World," Dean Martin

ORANGE YOU PAULIE GEE

Makes one 12-inch pie

You know I love wordplay. A lot of people ask me, "Aren't you Paulie Gee?" And I just happened to be searching for inspiration for a vegan dessert pie. Orange you glad I came up with this one? —PG

• •

1 round Neapolitan-Style Dough (page 19) or your favorite pizza dough (about ½ pound)

About ½ cup orange marmalade

¾ cup Cashew Ricotta (see page 99) or whole-milk ricotta cheese

Powdered sugar, for sprinkling

Prepare and heat your wood-burning/propane oven.

Place the dough on a pizza paddle and stretch it to about 12 inches. Use the paddle to transfer the pie to either the floor of your heated oven or a pizza stone. Bake for about 1 minute, until the crust is evenly brown and crisp.

Remove from the oven and evenly spread the crust with a layer of orange marmalade. Use a pastry bag or spoon to evenly space about 12 dollops of cashew ricotta over the pie. Sprinkle powdered sugar over the top, slice, and serve.

MOUSSE AU CHOCOLAT ORANGE

Serves 4 to 6

If toffee brickle (page 243) is my go-to dessert for big parties, this is Paulie's go-to for more intimate dinner parties. It's elegant and rich and always a hit. —MG

. . . .

4 large eggs, separated

1 cup semisweet chocolate chips (half a 12-ounce package)

3 tablespoons boiling water

2 tablespoons Grand Marnier orange liqueur

Whipped cream, for serving

Dark chocolate shavings, for serving

In the bowl of a stand mixer fitted with the whisk attachment or in a large bowl using a handheld mixer, beat the egg whites until stiff, 4 to 5 minutes.

Place the chocolate chips in a blender and blend on high for 6 seconds. Scrape the chocolate from the sides of the blender jar with a knife. Add the boiling water to the blender and blend on high for 10 seconds. Add the egg yolks and Grand Marnier and blend until smooth, about 3 seconds more.

A little bit at a time, use a rubber spatula to transfer the chocolate mixture to the bowl with the beaten egg whites and gently fold them together until completely incorporated.

Spoon the mousse into goblets, cover in plastic wrap, and chill in the fridge for at least 1 hour or up to 12 hours before serving. Garnish with whipped cream and chocolate shavings and serve.

MARY ANN'S DOUBLE-CHOCOLATE BROWNIES

Makes 9 brownies

I baked quite a bit when we lived in New Jersey, whether it was for our frequent dinner parties or for the kids' birthday parties and school events. I always preferred making desserts from scratch instead of using boxed mixes. You can really taste the difference. —MG

∙∙

⅓ cup salted butter, plus more for greasing

¾ cup sifted all-purpose flour

¼ teaspoon baking soda

¼ teaspoon kosher salt

⅓ cup granulated sugar

1½ cups semisweet chocolate chips

1 teaspoon pure vanilla extract

2 large eggs

½ cup walnuts, chopped (optional)

Powdered sugar, for dusting

NOTE

Don't be afraid to double the ingredients for a double batch of these double-chocolate brownies. Just bake the batter in a 9 x 13-inch pan.

Preheat the oven to 325°F. Grease a 9-inch square baking pan with butter.

In a large bowl, combine the flour, baking soda, and salt.

In a small saucepan, combine the butter, granulated sugar, and 2 tablespoons water. Bring to a boil over high heat, then remove from the heat. Add 1 cup of the chocolate chips to the saucepan, along with the vanilla. Stir until the chocolate has completely melted and the mixture is well combined and smooth.

Transfer the chocolate mixture to a large bowl and add the eggs one at a time, whisking well to combine after each addition. Slowly whisk in the flour mixture, then stir in the nuts (if using) and remaining ½ cup chocolate chips.

Pour the batter evenly into the prepared pan. Bake for 30 to 35 minutes, until a toothpick inserted into the center comes out clean. Remove from the oven and let cool completely before cutting into squares. Dust with powdered sugar and serve.

MIKE'S HOT HONEY SUNDAE

Serves 1

This is not so much a recipe as an amazing idea. As we've said, once we started putting Mike's Hot Honey on pies, it was only a matter of time before it found its way into everything else. —MG

•••

2 scoops of your favorite vanilla ice cream

Drizzle of Mike's Hot Honey

Handful of Candied Pecans (see page 151)

Do you really need instructions to know what to do here?

MRS. GEE'S TOFFEE BRICKLE

This is a very easy recipe that I always prepare at home for parties. It's totally addictive and almost impossible to eat just one piece. I also give it away in small packages as a holiday gift. The only time I don't make it is just for keeping around the house. We'd all be in trouble. —MG

`Makes one 11 × 16-inch pan`

1 sleeve Premium saltine crackers

1 cup (2 sticks) salted butter

1 cup packed light or dark brown sugar

2 cups semisweet chocolate chips (one 12-ounce package)

1 cup chopped walnuts (see Note)

NOTE

I use walnuts, but this would work with pecans or just about any other nut. If you're concerned about nut allergies, you can easily omit them, too.

Preheat the oven to 400°F. Line an 11 × 16-inch baking sheet with aluminum foil, making sure the foil completely covers the sides of the pan.

Place a single layer of saltine crackers on the prepared baking sheet. It might be necessary to break up a few of the crackers to evenly cover the entire pan.

In a small saucepan, combine the butter and brown sugar and bring to a boil over medium heat. Cook, stirring continuously, until it forms a smooth syrup, about 3 minutes. Immediately pour the syrup over the crackers, then place the baking sheet in the oven and bake for 5 minutes.

Remove the baking sheet from the oven and evenly distribute the chocolate chips on top. As the chocolate begins to soften and melt, use a silicone spatula to evenly spread it over the surface. Sprinkle the nuts on top, then place the brickle in the refrigerator for at least 30 minutes to cool completely and set. Break the brickle into pieces and store in an airtight container at room temperature for up to 1 week.

ITALIAN-STYLE CHEESECAKE

Makes one 9-inch cake

I've always enjoyed an Italian cheesecake, which is lighter and grainier than the cream cheese–based version. What I don't enjoy is the candied orange peel and other stuff that people tend to put inside. I've found that a bit of *pure* orange extract is perfect for adding the signature citrus element. Don't you dare use that imitation stuff. —PG

• •

1 ready-made unbaked pie crust for a 9-inch pan, such as Pillsbury refrigerated pie crust

1 (32-ounce) container whole-milk ricotta cheese

1 cup sugar

1 teaspoon pure vanilla extract

1 tablespoon pure orange extract

3 large eggs, beaten

Sliced fruit and/or marmalade, for topping (optional)

Preheat the oven to 375°F.

Line a 9-inch springform pan with the pie crust. It should extend a little way up the sides of the pan. Wrap the outside of the pan (bottom and sides) with aluminum foil and set it on a baking sheet to catch any drips. (This will also make cleanup *much* easier later.)

In a large bowl, stir together the ricotta, sugar, vanilla, orange extract, and eggs with a wooden spoon until well combined, then pour the mixture into the crust. Bake for about 1 hour 20 minutes, until the top is browned, then turn off the oven. Leave the cake in the oven until it collapses, about 15 minutes, then remove from the oven and let cool.

Transfer the cheesecake to the refrigerator and chill for at least 30 minutes or up to 6 hours before serving. When ready to serve, run a knife around the outside of the crust to help release it from the pan. Remove the springform ring from the pan and enjoy the cheesecake as is or with toppings like sliced fruit and/or marmalade.

Paulie Gee's Pizza Hit List

PG: How can I begin to explain this pizza hit list? Well, I guess it's best to start at the beginning.

MG: Paulie and I both grew up in Brooklyn, New York. My mom, Catherine, was the only single mother on our street after my dad passed away. She worked full-time, and since my grandmother lived with us, she was able to do all the day-to-day stuff, like cooking. Of course, my grandmother needed a break, too, so my mom would order pizza every Friday night from Krispy Pizza in Dyker Heights.

PG: My family lived in the Kensington neighborhood of Brooklyn. And Friday-night pizza must have been a lot of people's tradition, because I'd smell it all throughout our apartment building. But my family couldn't afford to buy any. We cooked all of our meals. My mom, Sally, kept a weekly list of all the meals she planned to make after working her full-time job.

MG: At my grammar school, students were allowed to go out to buy lunch since we didn't have a cafeteria. My friend Lori and I would walk a few blocks over to an Italian bakery and get a piece of square pizza for twenty-five cents. So basically, NYC-style slice pizza/bakery pizza was what I knew for a long time.

PG: Same. It all started with my first slice on McDonald Avenue at about the age of five. There was also a pizzeria on 13th Avenue in Borough Park called Gino's that made a really good Sicilian that

I used to measure all others against. The owner eventually moved to Staten Island and opened up another place that I went to visit as an adult, and his Siciilian tasted exactly the same as I remember. It was like discovering that a friend of yours who you thought had passed away was really alive.

Then I discovered coal-fired pizza at Totonno's in Coney Island in the mid-1990s. My mind was blown. I started to take our kids on pizza tours all around NYC, or search out the best pizza in other parts of the country during road trips.

By the way, I started embarking on pizza tours before there *were* any food/pizza tours. I'd drag family and friends from New Jersey into Brooklyn, have a slice or two at each place, and move on. I even organized a few tours with interested parties over Instagram. One year we had a five-borough pizza tour, and I thought we would literally bust at the end of that one. Now, it's become a professional business for a bunch of people, including our good friend Scott of Scott's Pizza Tours.

MG: When guests from out of town visit our locations, we always mention other pizzerias we know and like near the places they live. That's a lot of recommendations over the course of fourteen-plus years. The locations on the following page are the compiled results.

PG: There are no "bests," only "favorites." That phrase was coined by our friend and colleague Kelly Beckham, who owns Paulie Gee's Hampden in Baltimore, Maryland. We always give credit where credit is due.

Arizona
Phoenix
Pizzeria Bianco

Arkansas
Hot Springs
DeLuca's Pizza

California
Los Angeles
Naughty Pie
 Nature
Secret Pizza
Prime Pizza
Quarter Sheets
 Pizza

San Diego
Tribute Pizza

San Francisco
PizzaHacker
Del Popolo
Emilia's Pizzeria
Long Bridge
 Pizza Co.

Santa Barbara
Bettina

Colorado
Denver
Blue Pan Pizza
Pizzeria Lui

Nederland
Crosscut

Connecticut
New Canaan
Joe's Pizza

New Haven
Frank Pepe Pizze-
 ria Napoletana
Modern Apizza

Stamford
Colony Grill

West Haven
Zuppardi's Apizza

Florida
Miami
Lucali

Iowa
Des Moines
Fong's

Illinois
Chicago
Coalfire
Lou Malnatti's
Spacca Napoli
My Pie
Marie's

Louisiana
New Orleans
Pizza Delicious
Zee's
Ancora

Maryland
Baltimore
Joe's Squared

Ohio
Columbus
Harvest

Nevada
Las Vegas
Metro Pizza
Pizza Rock
Good Pie

Minnesota
Minneapolis
Pizzeria Lola
Hello

New Jersey
Elizabeth
Santillo's Brick
 Oven Pizza

Hoboken
Tony Boloney's

Hopewell
Nomad Pizza
 Company

Jersey City
Pizzeria Razza

Raritan
DeLucia's Brick
 Oven Pizza

Somerville
Prima Pizza
 Kitchen

New York
Brooklyn
Lucali
Joe's Pizza
Juliana's Pizza
L'Industrie Pizza
Motorino
Roberta's
Totonno's
Nino's Pizza
Wheated
The Za Report
 (Pop-Ups)

Elmont
King Umberto

Huntington
1653 Pizza
 Company

Manhattan
Joe's Pizza
Emmett's
Una Pizza
 Napoletana
Pizzeria San
 Matteo
Scarr's Pizza
L'Industrie Pizza
Patsy's Pizzeria
 (East Harlem)
Motorino
Mama's TOO!

Mamaroneck
Sal's Pizzeria

Pound Ridge
The Inn at Pound
 Ridge by Jean-
 Georges

Queens
Andrew Bellucci's
 Pizzeria
Filomena's

Staten Island
Joe & Pat's
Brothers Pizza

The Bronx
Louie & Ernie's

Williston Park
Gino's Pizzeria

Oregon
Portland
Scottie's Pizza
 Parlor
Apizza Scholls
Lovely's Fifty Fifty
Handsome

Pennsylvania
Philadelphia
Pizzata Pizzeria
Angelo's Pizzeria

Pizzeria Beddia
Circles + Squares
Pizza Shacka-
 maxon

Texas
Austin
Via 313

Multiple Locations
Cane Rosso

Washington
Seattle
Delancey
Dino's Tomato Pie

Washington, DC
All-Purpose
 Pizzeria
Andy's Pizza
Etto

Wisconsin
Milwaukee
Maria's Pizza

Racine
Wells Brothers

International
London, UK
Pizza Pilgrims

Naples, Italy
L'Antica Pizzeria
 da Michele
Sorbillo

Rome, Italy
Pizzarium Bonci
La Montecarlo

Spain
Grosso Napoletano
 (40+ locations)

Acknowledgments

First and foremost, I, Mary Ann, would like to thank my husband of forty-five years, Paulie Gee. I am so proud of you for stepping out of your comfort zone and starting this crazy journey when you were already fifty-six years old. Our life has changed immeasurably for the better. Besides fulfilling many of our dreams, we have been able to help others achieve their goals and dreams by starting small businesses of their own. Paulie, you have been nothing but fabulous with your contributions, especially your sharp wit regarding this project.

We have dreamt about writing this book for over ten years and always trusted that everything would line up when the time was right, and it did in a unique series of ways. If we were to thank everyone who has been a part of the success of the business and of this book, the list would be a book unto itself in length. Here is a mere start in acknowledging some of the people on that list.

To our children, Michael and Derek. You amaze us every day with your brilliance and kindness, which are shining mainstays in this crazy world. We know adjusting to our hectic calendars hasn't always been easy, but somehow, we always make it work! Of course, we must also mention our grandkids, who have given us so much joy and hope for the future.

To our parents: Though you all have been gone for so many years, you taught us many valuable lessons that we still carry today. We wish you could have been here to share this story with us, but we know you are always with us in spirit.

To the four other members of the "Five Guys," Jim, Cliff, Bill, and Rusty, and their spouses, Bess, Christine, Kathy, and Annie, thank you for supporting us through this journey. We are forever grateful.

To Mary Ann's besties, Maryann and Lori: Where would I be without your unconditional love and ears? You have always taken the time to listen, even when it was painful.

We would be remiss if we didn't mention our accountant and business manager, Nick. Thanks for putting up with our madness; as you know, we don't run a business like others do.

To the Shea family, Mary Ann's brothers, John and Gerard, and your children: Thanks for your love and support over the years. We especially want to mention Justin and Diane (Daniece & Danephew) for your unending commitment to us from the beginning of the Paulie Gee's adventure to this day.

To Mary Ann's cousins, Lori and Cheryl, and their families: Even though you are very removed cousins, you are really the sisters I never had. So happy we have remained so close since you were just little kids and in our bridal party forty-five years ago.

To all the other pizzeria owners who willingly and enthusiastically gave Paulie advice when we started, especially Chris Bianco, Mark Iacono, and Mathieu Palombino: Much of your insight helped to propel Paulie's vision.

To the pizza enthusiasts and influencers, many of whom we have known for years: We appreciate your willingness to spread the word about us and share our pizza.

Thanks to our original group of investors (mostly family and close friends) for believing in Paulie Gee's vision and investing your hard-earned dollars. Without you, we would not even be telling this story, as we didn't have any money to start a business.

To our terrific employees over the past fifteen years: You have inspired us to keep going despite tough times. Many of you have gone on to open your own places, and we couldn't be happier about that!

To our guests: We have enjoyed chatting and sharing stories. After all, life is an incredible, unending journey, and we are all part of a bigger picture.

To Colleen Kavanaugh, who helped us understand that this story should be told to inspire others to step out of their comfort zones and pursue their passions. Your assistance in documenting our history and submitting a proposal to agents we never heard back from was a blessing in disguise, even though we didn't know it at the time.

Thanks to Alex Penfold for helping us restart the proposal process a little later during the pandemic after we had finally moved back to Brooklyn permanently.

Serendipitously, we met Raquel Pelzel at 60 Greenpoint, and she suggested we contact Sarah Smith from the David Black Agency. Sarah, I couldn't be happier with your grace and poise in handling this book project.

Sarah also came up with a cowriter, Sarah Zorn, whom we knew from the early days. We had not been in touch for years but were featured in one of her books in 2012. Ironically, Sarah, you were the first to write about Mike's Hot Honey in the *Brooklyn Paper*, bringing this whole book idea full circle.

I ended up with a great team of people at Union Square & Co. (Caitlin Leffel, Renée Bollier, Amanda Englander, Lisa Forde, and Linda Liang) and eventually our food photography group (Matt Taylor-Gross, Brooke Deonarine, Spencer Richards, and Scotty Fletcher). You have all been extraordinary in your patience and kindness, especially since this is a new arena for us.

A picture is worth a thousand words, so last but not least, to the person who helped "write" this book with the pizzas in the photographs: Thank you, Logan Driscoll, for spending part of a week making all the wood-fired pies featured in the book. They all came out looking (and tasting) delectable!

Index